College: Why Should You Pay For It?

I Didn't

By

Charles J. Phillips

authorHOUSE™

1663 LIBERTY DRIVE, SUITE 200
BLOOMINGTON, INDIANA 47403
(800) 839-8640
WWW.AUTHORHOUSE.COM

First published by AuthorHouse 01/14/05

ISBN: 1-4184-3950-9 (e)
ISBN: 1-4184-3951-7 (sc)

Printed in the United States of America
Bloomington, Indiana

This book is printed on acid-free paper.

I would like to dedicate this book to my aunt, Karen Rawls and my mother, Retoin George. For if it had not been for that long car ride when both of you were explaining that I have a gift and I should share it, I never would have had the motivation to write this book. Thank you for your inspiration. Even though I haven't begun traveling the country to speak, this book is just one step towards that progress. You are very special to me and have boosted me to a level of which I never anticipated elevating to.

Table of Contents

Preface

There are a million and one reasons why you can go to college without having to pay a penny, and actually, in some cases get thousands of dollars back! This book will help you find those avenues and motivate you to go out and search venues, collect information, help others, organize ideas, lead, become active, and get results. When you have finished reading this text, you will know what types of finances are available, how to access these finances, and the time frame in which all of this should be done. You will be one of those students walking around campus everyday with the biggest smile on your face because you have ultimate value on your education, because you worked hard to get there and you know that you don't have to pay a penny for it, because you have enough awards that you have gotten extra money back. It can be done, and you will do it. The chapters in the book will help you achieve something that many feel is unimaginable. It is not, and you will see.

I. Setting The Perfect Foundation

"FEBRUARY 15th!"

"What do you mean February 15th, it's already the 5th!"

"Well if you want the scholarship, you need to fill out the application, write the essay, get three letters of recommendation, and have all of that postmarked by February 15th."

"Talk about pressure, deadlines, last minute. How in the world can I accomplish all of that by the 15th?" I thought to myself. "But it is a scholarship worth three thousand dollars. I guess I'll just put off everything else because that will help pay for books, and room and board. I need that money!"

This is the typical thought going through the mind of a person who waited too late to apply for a scholarship. But, ironically, there aren't many students who fall into this dilemma. I have done a lot of traveling and been in many summer educational advancement and college preparation programs. Combined with those two types of experience along with work experience, I have met a lot of intelligent, high scholastically achieving individuals who weren't in this dilemma. They actually pay or have paid for their entire education out of their own pockets! I always ask, "Why didn't you get any scholarships to help pay for college?"

Guess what the most popular answer was? "I didn't know where to look", and the second most popular answer was, "I didn't feel like filling out the application."

I plan to address both of these issues. The first is understandable, but for my peers that give me the latter answer, I usually give them a look that says, "Well I guess you have gotten what you deserve."

When you get a chance to indulge in what people your age in other countries and continents can only dream of, and do it for free, you must take advantage of that opportunity and put everything that you have into doing it. Unlike what most people say, *life is long,* and there will be ample time for you to play basketball, go to concerts, play cards, or whatever other excuse you can think of for not putting your time and effort into scholarship searching.

For any great work, you must create a foundation. The best way to get a scholarship is to have what the scholarship company is looking for. You don't have to be a 4.0 valedictorian who is the president of every organization at school. You don't have to be voted "most likely to succeed." You don't even have to be the most popular person in school. If you are any of the above, that is great and you also have an excellent light to shine to receive scholarships; but if you aren't, you also can shine and receive ample funding so you can go to college free. This is what you need to do. Everything that I am about to tell you is achievable, and it is possible to fix any low standings of education at any time in your educational career. I will explain what I mean by that after I give you the list of achievable goals.

When scholarship companies analyze your information, they look at four main sections: grade point average, ACT/SAT scores, letters of recommendation, and essay. The ideal grade point average is a 4.0; you should strive to make a 4.0 every semester that you are in school. Don't just say to yourself that you want to make a 4.0, actually study hard so that you can earn a 4.0. But if you don't, that is not a problem. For scholarships, aim your cumulative grade point average to be a 3.5 or higher. If you have that now, be sure to maintain it, because when they see that GPA, that automatically places you in good standings with the progress to success. If you don't have a 3.5 cumulative, try your hardest to get at least that. It is very hard to be turned down when you have a 3.5. If this is your senior year, and you don't have the GPA, do NOT let this be the reason that you pass a scholarship by. APPLY anyway you still may get it. Your chances are still high.

Test scores are important. I tell students to take both the ACT and the SAT, because if you score low

3

on one, and high on the other you can just submit the high score, which will give you the weight to still get a scholarship. On the ACT, strive for at least a 25. This is very attainable; you can do it. For the SAT, try to get at least an 1100. Both of these scores are excellent scores for these tests. When you get them and the companies/organizations see this, you will take yourself up one more notch to receiving a scholarship.

Do not think for a minute that you cannot get these test scores, because you can. The beauty of the ACT and SAT tests is that you can take them as many times as you want, and guess what? They only look at your best score. If you take the ACT and score a 10, and then take it again and score 20, and take it a third or fourth time and score 25 or better, the only score that counts is the 25 or better, and that is what will get you what you are searching for. Get both, the 25 and 1100, and you are worry-free. Do better than these two scores and you can almost write your own ticket.

Let me tell you a secret to scoring high on these tests: TAKE LATIN. Your high school should offer Latin as a foreign language. If you take that class and do well, you will definitely earn these scores. Your parents, your friends, and maybe even some of your teachers may tell you that it's a waste of time because no one speaks Latin anymore. Someone may even tell you that it is a "dead language". But as my college professor, Dr. Williams, once told me, "the dead provide for the living." All the difficult words that are used in the SAT/ACT are all of Latin base. Once you take that class and do well in it, you will be scoring in the 30s on the ACT and in the 1400s on the SAT.

Motivate yourself to do excellent in your classes and then when you get ready to take the tests, you will definitely score high on them.

Letters of recommendation weigh highly on your advancement. Everything else that is reviewed, with the exception of your personal essay, is basically a bunch of statistics: just numbers and letters. The recommendations are the only source or personal view that a board has to analyze you. Have at least five people write you a letter. Make sure you have two teachers, one principal, one counselor, one outside source who isn't a relative and if possible, get someone who has a Ph.D. For some reason, boards like to see someone of higher education recommending you. It serves as a personal motivation for you to finish undergraduate education and even continue higher than that.

One of the best letters of recommendation would be that of the individual or superior of a summer education program that you participated in. If you are applying for a mathematics/science scholarship and you were a participant in a mathematics/science type of program in the past, you would first definitely indicate that on your application; then go to the person who was at the top of the program, or even better, an individual you got to know very well that summer, and ask them if they would write you a letter. They are excellent resources because the review board will look at that and say, "Wow, this program coordinator was so impressed by this individual that they actually took the time out of their busy schedule to recommend them for our scholarship." That will move you up a lot of notches on the progress to achievement.

Once you have received your letters, make one copy of each before they sign it. This way, whenever you need to go back to them for another letter, you can just make a copy of the first letter and ask them to sign it again for the purpose of another scholarship you are applying for. When you do it this way, people will be glad to help you. It shows that you are organized and you also don't want to take up any more of their important time than is needed. Doing little things like that helps you in the long run, because you never know who that person knows. It may happen to you just as it did me.

I had already begun my first semester, and I went to the fiscal office to check on my account balance. I had received a scholarship that I didn't even apply for. Picture that! Someone I had been nice to in the past must have found out about a scholarship that their friend or maybe even their own personal organization was giving out, and they decided to send a scholarship to me. Wilder things have happened, but this is one occasion that adds to the pride of an individual.

The letters of recommendation give the review board a sort of second person kind of view. A lot of recommendations are kind of generic--"a great student, good leader." They get these all the time, and after a while they all start sounding the same. That is why I tell you to look over your letters of recommendation first and choose from your folder which recommendation(s) you are going to send--those you feel are the most notable.

I know you are sitting there thinking, "Well if 'great student, good leader' isn't good enough in a letter of recommendation, what is good enough?" Instead of saying "teacher, principal, family member, or friend" from now on I'll just address them as "recommender." When your recommender enlightens your audience (scholarship review committees) with words of grace, the board wants them to dig deep within their minds to explain situations where you were a great student. They would like to read about certain instances where you've displayed your great leadership skills, the outcome of what you have done, how it is relevant, and for what purpose you have "really" been recommended. Basically you want some specifics in your letter. "Great student, good leader" just says that the person was recommending you because you asked and they wanted to be nice. You want occurrences where the recommender is happy to write about you; you would like them to enjoy the time spent writing about you, and that is why you should be nice to all people.

The letters of recommendation are ways of viewing you through another person's eyes. The ACT/SAT and cumulative grade point averages are just statistical analyses of your average to below-average work effort. The reason I say "average to below-average" is because most high school work is not fun, and it is proven that you do your best work when you are enjoying what you are doing. If you don't enjoy it, then you will not work as hard on it as you should, and you begin to fall in the average to below-average work level. All of these statistics can be used to your advantage. So even though they are only statistics, try to maintain the work ethic of "above average" every day so you can keep your GPA up and do well on the tests.

The essence of the application is the essay. This is the only place in the whole entire application where a review committee actually gets a taste of your personality. It is true that not everyone likes writing, but just imagine you are writing, for example, a five hundred word essay for one thousand dollars. That means you are going to get paid two dollars for each word you put in that essay. Now don't think that you will get more money if you write more words, it doesn't work that way. Just make sure that you pour your heart into it. Don't spend so much time drudging over what you want to say. Look at the topic; think about it for 30 minutes at most, and then begin writing. Nine times out of ten, the topic of the essay will be something about future goals, perspectives on life or, in a low percent of cases, a reflection of yourself through the company's aim/purpose.

When you are writing the essay, read it over and make sure you are saying what you are really trying to say. You may even want to ask a friend to read it, but don't tell them what it is for. After your friend reviews it, ask them to explain to you how they perceive it. If that is how you want the board to receive it, don't change a thing, but if your friend explains something that is totally off, you may want to change a few things in your essay.

You want your essay to be written in a way that after the review board reads it, they are all impressed. Be clear on what you say, because you do not want anyone confused. They will be thinking about your work, but instead of them thinking, "That was an excellent essay," they will be thinking, "That was a confusing piece of junk." You want them to read the essay and continue talking about yours while they have already moved on to next application. They should go home thinking, "Wow, that student really impressed me, I understood what they were talking about in the essay, it made sense, and they really seem motivated to achieving their goals." It isn't difficult to do and I will explain how.

Future goals are what I personally feel is the most popular topic for scholarships. I would say that out of 50 essays I have had to write, 35 of them were about my goals. Before you even get the essay topic--even now as you are reading this book--think about what you want to do in life. Are you a creative person? Do you want to produce a new product? Are you a person who likes to fine tune products, take a product that has already been out on the market and make it better? Do you like to work in groups or do you like to work alone? What is your best working environment? Would you rather have a quiet corner in the library or a loud lunchtime hallway by your locker? All of these things that are in your everyday life are actually the foundation for your future.

If you don't mind staying up all hours of the night studying, you may like research, or maybe even emergency surgery. If you are a person who likes to be finished with work at a certain period of time every day, you may be more of a nine-to-five type businessperson, or maybe even a stock market type of person. If you like working with people and enjoy a lot of free time, you may want to think about becoming a teacher. Whatever you like to do, think about that and write it in your essay.

Be expressive and elaborate when you write. Indicate specifics about your future. Even if none of the reviewers can relate to what you want to do, your elaboration will give them an understanding, open their minds to something new; they will be able to see where you are planning to go with your life.

For example, look at these two sections of sample essays:

Essay #1:

"My long-term goal is to invent something that can help people out. I've always liked helping people and creating new things. Even though a lot of people will tell me that it is impossible, I still am going to do it, and I'm going to make this world a better place..."

Essay #2:

"First I plan to major in chemistry in college. I still haven't decided where I want to go yet, but I've narrowed it down to the University of Michigan and Johns Hopkins. After I get my Ph.D., I plan to do research on asthma. I know that it is a disease and it is said to be incurable, but I am going to find a cure. It may take twenty to thirty years of dedicated research, but I am ready for the trials and errors of my life to find a cure because treatments just aren't enough anymore..."

Even if both essays were five hundred words, the student that wrote the second essay would get the scholarship. The first one was very general, without specific details. It sounded like the student has dreams, but wasn't particularly sure what they actually wanted to do; they weren't detailed at all. The second excerpt had more specifics: chosen major, choices of universities; they had a definite idea of what they wanted to pursue, and they sound dedicated. If I had a choice between the two, I would choose the second student.

I realize that you as a student may not have a definite idea of what you want to do in college. The average college student changes their major about five times before they graduate. It's a fact that you will have a lot of thoughts going through your head about your future, and that is good. When you have more than one idea, you can change your mind. You will have a little bit of background on that subject and you can expand on that. When you write your essay, you can either choose one of your ideas or indicate all of them.

Whichever you choose, make sure you are detailed. I can't stress that enough; explain to these people what you want to do, and the route you plan to take to pursue it. If you want to include more than one, that is fine, just make sure that you are detailed in all of them. You don't necessarily have to include a time by which you plan to have your goals reached, but if you can, that would be good too.

The other popular essay subject deals with the company. Let's say, for instance, you apply to for a mathematics scholarship from a mathematics book company. Their topic may be, "Write a seven hundred fifty word essay describing the mathematics courses you have taken and how they affect your life." You may come across this type of essay for a wide range of subjects. If you get a topic of this kind, make sure that you write on that specific topic. Sometimes these seem very difficult because you may not see yourself relating to the topic.

Whatever the case may be, take a little while to think it over, and even if you have no idea of how this topic relates to your life, start writing something. You can go through it later and decide what you want to keep in it and what you want to leave out. If you get a topic like, "Describe how marine biology affects your life" and you don't have any idea what marine biology is, look it up, do some research. Remember, you are trying to get a college education for free. You need to practice your research skills anyway, since you are going to be in college in a year or so. Use all the knowledge you have gained to write the essay. Make sure that it makes sense, and proofread and change it until you feel it is noteworthy. You can achieve this; don't think for one second that anything is too difficult to achieve or that it will take too long to finish, or that you won't even get the scholarship. Don't let any of those ideas enter your mind. You are worthy of the scholarship and you *will* get it.

There is a very important lesson to be learned in the situation that you get a scholarship for a specific major--let's use engineering for an example--you get an engineering scholarship and then you get to school and realize that engineering is not the major for you. Even if you risk losing the scholarship, if you feel strongly that you would rather have a different major, change your major. Just make sure that you really want to do it. If you lose that scholarship, apply for other scholarships pertaining to your new major. If you get in your new major and decide you want to go back to engineering, change back. Then get in touch with the company and explain to them that you decided to go back to engineering and ask if they will reconsider your case and reinstate the scholarship.

You have to set a very strong foundation for yourself. There is not a set "perfect" time to begin your foundation. It can start when you are in elementary school, middle school, or even high school. If you are a person who hasn't been in school for a long time and have decided to go back and get your degree, you can begin setting your foundation today.

My strongest recommendation is to start during your sophomore year in high school. You have gotten the bugs of "finally being in high school" out of your system and you are ready to get down to business. What you should do now is bring your grade point average up. If you have a 4.0 GPA, just try to maintain it, but if you don't, aim for that. You should aim for a 4.0 every semester in school. I still try to get a 4.0 GPA every semester, and when I get into graduate school, I will continue the tradition of making a 4.0 my goal. Do not let anyone tell you that you cannot achieve this. You are an excellent student and you should always feel this way. There will always be people who say that you can't do something, but you cannot let their words affect your life, or your education.

Now that you are a tenth grader, you need to take the SAT/ACT tests either in the fall or spring. I recommend the fall, because this way you can take it in the spring if you need it, and you will always have your eleventh grade year to make up for any low scores you get in the tenth grade. If you wait until your eleventh grade year, you only have those two semesters to try to achieve the goals previously stated. There are sessions that you can participate in to help you prepare for the tests. It is up to your discretion if you would like to take part in them.

I would say participate in the program because you can never be too prepared for those tests, you can only be very well prepared. There is also an opportunity to have the fees for both ACT/SAT tests waived. To qualify for the fee waiver, you must (1) register with a paper application form or online (not by phone), (2) be a high school junior or senior, and (3), must meet the economic requirements as listed on the fee waiver form.

While in the tenth grade, start thinking about what you want to major in when you get to college. The best way to do this is to think about what courses you enjoy, and do some research on some of the majors that may correlate with those subjects. If you like history and social studies courses, you should look into becoming a lawyer, sociologist, psychologist, psychiatrist, or maybe even an investigator. If you like mathematics and science, you should look into the different engineering disciplines, pre-med, accounting or maybe even physics. If you like talking to people, you should look into radio broadcasting, business/marketing, or even international trade. If you like computers, you should look into computer engineering, computer programming, or Web design.

There are all kinds of different majors that correlate with what you like; just sit down and take about ten to fifteen minutes and try to answer this question: "If I could have any job in the world, what would it be?" Another good question to try to answer is, "What job would I like to do for at least 30 years?" When you answer these questions, you will begin to see what types of things you like to do and you can choose your major from that.

In the eleventh grade you should begin doing research on colleges and universities. Look at some of the rankings that are done. *U.S. News* magazine is a great place to start. They put a ranking out every year for each major. You may not find a school that you are interested in on the list, but rankings are good ways to jog your memory to what schools you may want to go to. If you are thinking about going to a Historically Black College or University, http://www.hbcu-central.com has information on all the HBCUs.

When searching for a university, the first item you **must** think about is, "Does this school have my major?" If it does not, then you can automatically rule that school out. You will probably be receiving a lot of mail now from all kinds of universities. Don't be surprised when you come home from school and your mailbox is full of applications, brochures, letters, and other little things that universities send students as solicitation. Don't be fooled though; there are some schools that want you particularly and there are others that just mail out paperwork to every student who is on a certain list. I used to go through all the mail that I got and throw away the letters I received that weren't personally signed. You will receive numerous letters; the majority of all you receive are just stamped with a person's name, or even photocopied. That takes out all of the personalization from the actual letter.

The only way I would have ever kept any of those letters would have been if one of the letters had been from a school that I specifically wanted to go to. Maybe it was luck or even irony, but whatever the case, I didn't get a stamped letter from any of the schools I had desired. Now if you have received mail from a school that stamped the letter, but they have your major and you are interested in that school, by all means, proceed in researching that university. You need to think of a way to filter out schools so that you won't spend all of your time looking for a school and not doing your work in high school.

Along with majors that a school offers, you should also look at the location and size of the university. Decide if you want to go to a big school or a small school. Michigan State University is about a ten-minute drive from where I grew up. There are at least forty thousand students at State, and it is in the north, which means that there are cold, snowy winters. Is that environment adequate for you? Some of the classes have up to five hundred students enrolled, but the university has a lot of resources for studying, and there is a cafeteria in almost every dormitory. They have co-ed dorms and they have a huge library. There's a mall down the street and all kinds of fast food places and stores up and down the main block. The campus is so big that they have their own bus system.

The school is in the Big Ten, so all the football and basketball games are fun and packed. They have concerts every once in a while, and it has a good reputation for just about all majors. On the other hand, Prairie View A&M University, where I currently attend is a Historically Black University located near Houston, Texas that has about seven thousand students; the weather is nice all year round (except for a few rainy days). At our school, there is only one cafeteria, the football team has only won about seven games in the last ten years, classes range from 10 to 150 students, everybody knows everybody, the closest store is a ten minute drive, the closest fast food restaurant is ten minutes too, the fraternities and sororities are a big part of campus life, it's very friendly, people are always speaking to you, and it's known mainly for the good engineering and nursing programs.

Money shouldn't be an issue because you will be getting your college paid for no matter where you go. But just to give you an example, MSU is about fifteen thousand dollars a year for *in-state* students and PVAMU is about eight thousand for *out-of-state* students and only four thousand for in-state. You should take into account everything about a university before finally settling down to your chosen few, and then based around them, begin applying.

You need to choose three to seven schools that you would like to attend. The reason being, you may find something out about one of the schools that you don't like and you may change your mind. The possibility is very slim, but there is a small chance that you may not get into the school that you want to attend; this way, you will have a backup plan. Once you've chosen the schools that you want to go to, contact the admissions office and find out how you can get the application fee waived. You never know, there may be stipulations that you fall into for the waiver and this will make it less expensive for you when it comes time to apply.

You have until the end of the summer between your junior and senior years to decide, because you won't be applying until you are a senior. The fall and spring semester of your junior year, you should also be trying to fine tune yourself to getting those ACT/ SAT scores up. If you haven't gotten that 25 or eleven hundred, don't give up, you can achieve it; just take them again and try your best. On the SAT you are penalized for guessing. So if you are on a question and you completely do not have a clue to which is the correct answer, skip that question. You are not graded on the questions that you don't answer. Your final score is calculated from an algorithm that includes the total number of questions you answered correctly and the total you answered incorrectly. But don't do anything crazy like only answering one question on the whole test; you definitely won't get a fifteen hundred (the highest possible score) if you do that. The ACT test, on the other hand, is scored differently than the SAT.

On the ACT you are not penalized for guessing, your score is based <u>only</u> on the number of correct answers. So it is recommended that you answer every question on that test.

Along with bringing up your test scores and fine tuning your list of colleges that you want to go to, you should spend your spring semester visiting colleges. Instead of going to any "big time" place for spring break, or even instead of sitting on your butt at home in front of the TV bored all break, see if your parents or friends want to go on a road trip to visit different colleges. I am the youngest in my family, and my brother and sister wanted to go to different colleges. My parents were always ready to road trip and visit campuses, so just imagine how many different schools I have visited. For spring break my junior year, one of my teachers who was close to the family took me to North Carolina so that I could visit North Carolina A&T State University. Her daughter went to A&T. We were going to drop off her daughter's new car which also would allow me time to view the campus.

Take advantage of any opportunity that you have to visit schools. That is the best way that you will ever get to know how good a school is for you. Many times, you get tours from some of the faculty who work on that campus. They are very good resources, but I would recommend that you ask the students on campus to give you a small tour (if it's a small university); but if you are on a large campus, just ask some students questions about the school that you are curious about.

When I went to PVAMU for the first time, the campus seemed very dead. The student who was giving us a tour spoke very highly of the educational system of this elaborate university, but out of the blue, I asked him, "Do y'all ever have parties?" I'm not saying go and find out about the social life of every campus you visit, but you should ask a few questions about that, because the true essence of college life is both educational and social. Without both you would go crazy, so make sure you ask any questions about anything that you are curious about. College students are the best resources, because they already are where you are trying to be.

Senior year: this is the time when everything comes together. You need to send in all your college applications either the first or second week of your senior year. I know that it is hard, because the first couple of weeks of school, counselors are still trying to put students in classes, you're still trying to figure out what classes you want, and you begin to get a case of senioritis. You have to buckle down and take care of business. Get all of them filled out <u>before</u> school starts, so that once school starts, you can get your transcripts and mail off your applications right away. When you do this, you alleviate yourself from a lot of problems. Now you don't have to worry about anything being late. You can check to make sure they got all of your paperwork, so that even in the event that your paperwork gets lost in the mail, you still have ample time to send another application in.

You should also make a copy of EVERYTHING: your application, essay and recommendations after you've finished it; that way, if anything happens to your paperwork, you can just fill out another application word for word from your copy and make copies of the other paperwork to send in. The most important reason you should send in your materials early is to open the door to that specific university's scholarships. Make sure you contact the admissions office in the summer to find out if they have a "general" scholarship application for the university, or if you have to go through the department that you plan to enter. They may send you a financial aid packet, but what you *really* want are some papers that deal specifically with scholarships.

If you don't get any help from admissions, ask if they have a "scholarship office." If they do, then get in contact with them; they will definitely have what you need. In the event that the admissions office doesn't help you and there is not a scholarship office, or on very rare occasions, there is a scholarship office, but they do not properly help you, contact the financial aid department. This department is different from the scholarship office because it deals with **all** financial aid (i.e. loans, grants), whereas the other deals solely with scholarships, and that is what you want--"free money."

By the middle of the fall semester of your senior year, October/November, you should have all the deadlines, applications, or at least knowledge of where to get information for all the scholarships that you plan on applying for. The majority of them are usually due at the end of January or even the end of February. What you need to do is begin filling out these applications, getting letters of recommendation, and organizing everything that you have, so that you can have your application ready to send a month before the deadline.

If you'll notice, I always say that you should send information early. The reason I say this is because there is a possibility that your paperwork could be lost in the mail, and if you wait until the week before the deadline and your paperwork gets lost, you have no time to fill out another application and mail it in. But you also need to make copies of all finished paperwork so that in case it does happen, you will have a backup packet to revert to. I had an application due February 15, just about five months ago. I sent the application on January 30; I only had a two-week time period, which wasn't very much. I forgot to do something very important. I didn't call to make sure they received my application. Always contact the scholarship review board by phone or e-mail. They will provide you with some kind of contact information; make sure that your information was received. At the beginning of June, since I hadn't heard from the company, I finally decided to call. (Keep in mind they inform the scholarship recipients in April or May.) **This was very late**. I spoke with the supervisor of the program and he informed me that they had not received my application. Don't let this happen to you; that was two thousand five hundred dollars that went down the drain because I made the mistake of not contacting this company.

Also around this time, you should be getting letters back from the universities (October-early December, for schools that are very organized). Along with your acceptance letters, you will also be provided with scholarship opportunities the school has for you, and other background information about admissions that you need to know. When you get this information, you have to finally make a decision which school to choose from all the acceptance letters that you've received. You have to mail your acceptance back to the school to let them know if you are still serious about attending that university. You cannot be penalized if you send an acceptance back but you later change your mind, so if you are stressed out over which school you want to go to, send more than one back, but if you have decided on one--which in most cases you will have--send your letter, sit back, relax, and wait for your scholarship letters.

Don't fall into the trap of not taking high school seriously. Don't forget, you still have one more semester of high school to finish. You really want to have all of your college business taken care of by the end of February. When you know that you are accepted into a college and that you have enough scholarships to pay for school, it's a lot easier on your mind. You can focus on **school** first! But you can also think about where you'll be going for spring break, what you're going to wear to prom, how you plan on spending the summer before college. All of these activities are vital to you at this point in time, and it wouldn't be fun if you had to worry about how much you or your parents are going to have to come up with out-of-pocket next semester. If you follow the plan that I have set, you will be in good shape and easy spirits, because you will be so excited that you don't have to pay for school; everything else will be a breeze.

You may not realize how big of a deal paying for college is, but here is a scenario that may help. Imagine this: you are at college and they hand you a bill for twelve thousand dollars; this is before you add on books and the hundred to two hundred dollars you will spend on snacks, and other stuff that you want to put in your room. You will have to spend about thirteen thousand dollars on all of this stuff. Let's say, for instance, you do not have any scholarships at all. Where is the money going to come from? The deadline for the first installment is coming fast, and if you don't have enough money to pay for that first installment, they will drop you out of the system. YOU WILL BE KICKED OUT OF SCHOOL, and this happens to a lot of people because of poor planning.

Let's just say for the sake of argument that your parents pay the thirteen thousand dollars, but they are struggling to do that. How much money do you think is going to be left for you to enjoy? What if you have to have Christmas with no presents? It could happen because of all of these college bills, which are added on to the bills your parents already pay. Do you think your parents can afford to spend thirteen thousand dollars on you right now?

Now, look at the opposite scenario. It's February, your last semester of your senior year, you have enough scholarships to cover that thirteen thousand and you will also get one thousand dollars back. You and your parents know this. You have just saved your parents ***thirteen thousand dollars***, spring break is coming up, you want to go to Cancun, and you want that nice dress or the cool tuxedo that you saw for prom. Your parents can afford all of this stuff because they don't have to pay for college. You see a nice car that you want, and you tell your parents you have to have one for college; you have a much better chance getting that car now because those are one-time expenses and your parents can handle that. (You may have to get a job to keep up the maintenance.) Think about it, which scenario would you rather have?

Set your foundation so that you can enjoy your last semester, and semesters to come. You will have a lot of expenses to cover before college and while you're in college. You aren't always going to want to eat in the cafeteria. Sometimes you're going to want to go to the mall or the movies. All of these are expenses that you have to think about. If there's a big party at a school 30 minutes away, you have to pay for gas and that party. If you get a cell phone, you have to pay a monthly bill for that. Everybody can always use new clothes.

You have to take all of this into account when you are thinking about the cost and expenditures of college life. All of the stories I have presented are real; they are not made up. I know people who have been kicked out of school because they needed one more day past the deadline before they could pay their installment. I know people who have had a Christmas with no presents, but I also know folks who drive a new Lexus, and have top-of-the-line clothing. I'm not saying that a scholarship is going to help you afford all of these things, but managing your money will, and a college education is a major step to life in the real world, and it is the best place to acquire money managing skills.

The foundation is the most important part of any success; it is what you build upon and it is where the beginnings lay. Usually laying the foundation is the hardest part. You can ask anyone you know who you feel has a successful career, a successful story, or even someone who has just done one successful thing in life, and they will tell you how strong of a foundation they have. The glitz and glamour is always the aftermath of the work and diligence. Both can be acquired, and they will be once you have finished setting your foundation.

Before you begin looking in books and talking to people, before you begin trying to get those four point grade point averages, you have to do something that is very important. If there was anything that deserves to earn the title of urgency, this is it. You must get your mind right. It may sound quite trite or maybe even to some extent cliché, but if you seriously want to go to school and get enough scholarships that you will be able to have extra money in your pocket, you have to seriously get in the correct mind state and mentality.

I can tell you what it is and how it feels when you have it, but you and only you can take yourself to that level. Nobody else can do it. Not your mother, not your father, not your teachers, not even your friends can influence you to get your mind right. People can motivate, stimulate, and even inspire you to limits that are unknown, but without the right mentality, once that person stops talking to you, all the inspiration, all the stimulation, and all the motivation will just wither away, and you will still be stuck at ground zero with nothing.

The right mentality is a feeling. Well, actually it is more than just a feeling; there is a sensation about you that no one can quite figure out. It is almost as if you have such zeal that you glow as bright as the green glow sticks kids carry around trick or treating at night around Halloween time. You will not let anyone tell you anything because your mind has been set on achieving a certain goal and you will not give up until that goal has been reached.

When I say your mind has been set, I do not mean that there are just thoughts about it, constantly circling around in your brain and it seems like something good to do. No, you will actually have a focus and just about everything else that surrounds you does not matter. This is to the point where you have decided to get this money and you will not rest until it has been received. When you gain this mentality, you will be at the point where if you get a letter back from a company that says you were denied, you will have enough boldness to pick up your phone and call them and ask why. "Why did I not get the scholarship? I know that I am qualified." You are bold, but you are also smart enough to understand that you must be polite with the people you get in touch with, and that you should speak directly with the person who writes the checks or the person who tells the other person whom to write the checks to. Usually the middle-man or the secretary, will not have all the information that you require. They may try to get you to leave your name and number, in which, you may not receive a phone call back, or they may just tell you to try again next year. In this case, they are just blowing you off. If you speak directly to the person in charge of the program, you are more likely to receive an honest response as well as an opportunity to receive the money in the case that there was a mix-up with your paperwork. This is more than just a thought, it is really more than a zone, this mentality is something greater than you have experienced before, but the glory of it is that you can develop this mentality and it will help you go far in life.

The way you do this is to center your mind on your goal. "I want to go to school for free. As a matter of fact, I want to earn so many scholarships that I have at least one thousand dollars extra to spend on something else I may want to do." Put that thought in your head and keep thinking it. You want that embedded so deeply within you that you start working at it, nothing will be allowed to stand in your way. It should become you, and when I say that, I mean it will not even be a thought anymore, it will become a fact and you will be the one to prove it. You will prove it to yourself, prove it to all those who believe in you, and prove it to all those who don't think you are worth anything; those who have put you down and said this is something that you cannot achieve.

I love it when people try to say that there is something that I cannot do, and when I finally do it, I can just look them in the face and say, "Look, what I've done." When I was a freshman in college, a lot of us were talking about getting internships (summer jobs with big companies that deal directly with your major). I told them that I wanted to get an internship that paid ten thousand dollars over the summer. You know what they did? They laughed. There were about 30 of us, and after I said that, all 29 of them were laughing in my face at my idea. Once they finally got up from the ground and wiped their tears from their faces from laughing so hard, they were like, "Charles, come on man, you know you cannot get an internship that pays ten thousand dollars. It is just not going to happen." Guess what? This summer I have an internship paying me three thousand six hundred eighty five dollars a month, and I am working for three months. I will let you do the mathematics on that one.

You can achieve your goal just like I did. I made it a fact in my mind that I was going to get an internship paying at least ten thousand dollars along with getting enough scholarships to go to school for free. Once you make it a fact in your mind, you are not going to have to worry about anything. You will constantly work at achieving your goal. Every time you see a book or an article, a Web site or a newsletter about scholarships, you will attack and you will get what you are searching for.

Make what you want a fact within yourself. Right now, decide that you are going to do it, and that no one will be able to stop you from doing it. When I say no one, I even mean me. Don't let anything that I say stop you from achieving your goal. If you don't have the GPA or test scores that I have stated you should achieve, don't let that stop you. If you don't really even know if you want to go to college, don't let that stop you. Think of every reason why you don't think you will be able to achieve this goal, and use all that negativity as positive fuel for your search. That is your motivation; let that fuel and that fact take you on the journey to a free education.

II. Where to Look

Enter the world of free money. Imagine posters of people with thousands of dollars in their hand, looking happy as can be, with signs under their faces that say "THIS COULD BE YOU!" It can be and it will be if you flow down the correct rivers to researching and finding your scholarships. There will be many times when you are going to find scholarships that are not relevant to you. The application may state, "must be a college freshman or sophomore". I'll tell you from experience, for every one of those that you run into, there are going to be three more that say, "high school senior or entering college freshman". These are the ones you need to attack.

Through your researching, you will find scholarships that may only be for people with unique physical attributes like being left-handed. If you are left-handed, this is a perfect situation for you; apply for it, do your best on your application so that you can get it. The mode of thinking that I want you to be in from this point forward is, "I AM NOT PAYING FOR COLLEGE". Say that to yourself. Refuse to give up the battle of your search, stride forward and at a hard pace to find many applications you can apply for.

If you are at a point where you aren't sure what you want to major in, apply for scholarships that are for all the majors that you are considering. On the application where it states "Major: _____", put down the major that the application is designated for. Before I continue, let me give you an example of what I just said. Say for instance you are thinking about majoring in chemistry, but you are also thinking about sociology. These are two totally different majors and you will find a number of scholarships that are looking for students who want to major in chemistry and a number of scholarships specifically for students majoring in sociology. On all these, it never fails, even though the application specifies what major the scholarship is for, there will be a space provided where you are to fill in your proposed major. If you haven't decided between those two majors, collect applications for both of them. Make sure you don't mix these up, because on all the sociology applications you are going to put down **sociology** for the major, and for all the chemistry applications, put down **chemistry**.

Now I need to give you fair warning, there will be a time when you have to make a decision on a major, but by then you will already have received the scholarships. When you finally enter college and choose one of the majors, you *may* lose all of the scholarships from the other major. This is understandable. Think about it, why would an organization, say the American Chemical Society, for example, support a student who is majoring in sociology? It just doesn't make sense because they are a foundation of chemistry. **BUT**, and I seriously stress that but, DO NOT let that be your reason for not applying. Apply for everything that you may want to study. Just imagine if you applied for and got all sociology scholarships and then you got to school and decided to do chemistry, you wouldn't have any money to pay for school. A lot of the scholarship boards would take your scholarship away because when you sign your name on that application, you are saying you are going to major in that area. When you change your mind, you are breaking the agreement, but it is worth it because if you don't cover all of your bases, you may lose out on something. So apply for everything you find.

I know you are sitting there right now thinking, "OK Charles, you've told me how to set my foundation to get scholarships, what grades I need, what I should aim for on the test, and the time frame I should do all of this in, but you have forgotten to include the most important part. WHERE do I start looking for scholarships?" Well, the "where" is the easy part. You should look everywhere and I do mean everywhere, because nine times out of ten, a scholarship is right under your nose and you don't even realize it. To be more formal, there are five main categories of places to start looking, but if you find any other resources besides these that help you, use those too. Use everything in your grasp that can help you achieve your goals, and access as much information as you can. The five main categories are: colleges, books, companies, organizations, and the all famous Internet.

Before I begin telling you where to look, I must, it is my duty to take this time out to warn you. This is sort of a public service announcement. You will be invited to hear different speakers sometime between your junior and senior year. Don't think that you will be left out, because it is going to happen. They will try to convince you to pay them around three hundred dollars or some ridiculous figure, and they promise to take all of your personal information and put a package together filled with scholarship information. It sounds tempting, but what they don't tell you is that they don't get you any money; all they get you is the applications, and they will try to mess with you by saying they have access to scholarships that you won't be able to find. If it takes secret access to get a certain scholarship, you don't even want that money anyway.

If you would like to hear them speak, that's fine, but I recommend that you don't buy their services. I have to take the time out to say sorry to you speakers, but your services aren't worth it. You, the student, can do the work yourself and you will have all applications that apply strictly to you. That three hundred or so dollars can be used somewhere else that is more productive for your future. I have never met a person who has said they received scholarships by using one of those speakers' services. Why pay all that money to get something that is not a "sure thing"? I don't buy their advertisement and you shouldn't either. You may commit to that and find the scholarships that they have found for you don't even apply to you. How would you feel then? Don't do it.

I believe I referred you to college as a source in the first chapter. It is very important that you become familiar with your college scholarship office or financial aid office (for universities that do not have a scholarship office) because they will be your best friends if you are nice to them. There's a saying that isn't always true, but in the case of getting in good with your scholarship office personnel, it definitely stands true: "It is not always what you know, but who you know." You may not know where every scholarship is, and it is really impossible for you to know because there are so many different scholarships out there. But if you get in close with the people who work in the scholarship office, you will always be the first to know about a scholarship that applies to you. They will always keep their eye out for you, and that is definitely a plus, because even when you are in class studying, they are constantly receiving scholarship applications from different groups.

Just imagine getting back to your room after class with a message on your answering machine saying, "Come over to the scholarship office, some applications came in and I see a few that fit you perfectly." To get a message like that is a privilege, because they don't call too many people. It's truly your duty to make sure you know what's going on in their office, but when you get cool with them, they won't mind taking two minutes away from their day to give you a call and let you know what's going on. Make sure that you know them very well.

When you send your college applications off in the first or second week of your senior year, you should also have a scholarship application for each university that you are applying to. If you don't have one, you can get these faxed or mailed to you from the individuals in the various scholarship offices. These are the applications that help you get "full rides," so they are very important. You should take all of your scholarship applications very seriously and take your time filling them out, but you need to give special attention to this particular application because they are usually automatically renewable if you are awarded.

When I went to North Carolina A&T and Prairie View, the first place I visited was the scholarship office. I spoke to the person who was in charge of the office. I always like to speak to the top representative because they know exactly what is going on. Usually when you talk to that person's secretary or even the student worker, you will be led in the wrong direction because these people usually don't have a clue as to what is really happening. You may get there and talk to the secretary and you're told, "Oh we don't have scholarship applications for entering freshmen," and most of the time when you get this type of information that isn't helpful, it's not that they are trying to be rude or mean, they just don't know. Instead, when you approach the secretary, ask to speak to the person in charge of the office, because they will be able to help you.

When you visit a university bring your transcript with you too, and it is better when you do not go in large groups. When I say large groups, I'm talking about college tours that some high schools go on. The tours are good, but when 50 people walk into the scholarship office, there is no way that you are going to get the same personal attention and proper information that you can get when you go there by yourself, or just you and your parents. The information that you will receive when it's just you or you and your parents will be a lot more detailed and specific to your needs than if you go there in a large tour group. When you go in large college tour groups, a lot of the information that you need specifically is skipped over because they will be trying to address the group as a whole to provide a more broad view.

At A&T, I went to the office by myself, but at PV, I was with my father. I recommend taking your transcript because usually they can give you an estimate of what types of scholarships you qualify for; even though it's still only your junior year of high school, this is a motivational tool that will activate your mind to increase your grades and to try to get a better offer than what you were quoted at. It is also good because they have a better chance of remembering your face or name when your application comes, and it will go to them, so be nice. They see hundreds to thousands of applications each day, but don't underestimate the power of your personality in the short time of a conversation you have with that representative. A good conversation is like a gold game, they are both business ventures and can both produce positive outlooks for your future.

If you don't get a chance to actually go to the college and personally speak with someone face to face, make sure you contact them, more than once if you have to, but make sure you get one of their scholarship applications either mailed or faxed to you and that you know exactly what needs to be sent in with it.

When you send in the application for college, make sure you send in the scholarship application too because the earlier they realize that you need the money and that you qualify for the money, the better chance you have of getting a full ride. Most students wait until the middle or near the end of the fall semester of their senior year to mail off their application, and there are others who get their application in just before the deadline. These are usually the students who don't get money. Don't fall into this category.

There is a myth that you shouldn't send in your application too early because they wait until the deadline before they start sending students' acceptance letters and scholarship offers. This is entirely false. I received my acceptance letter and scholarship offer in October of my senior year from one of the universities I applied for, and their deadline was long after December. Most students were still trying to figure out what school they wanted to go to and I already had my offer. You can too. Being an early bird is always the best because it shows initiative, ambition, and leadership. Go that route; it is a winning one.

Aside from scholarships of that university, the scholarship office will also know about other scholarships from companies and organizations that send them directly to the school. There are many companies that endow schools with millions of dollars. Most of that money goes toward modernizing the university and making sure that the students have a top-of-the-line studying environment and high quality resources, but some of the money is also allocated to scholarships. Don't be discouraged from applying because you think they are only for students who are already in college, because they aren't. Those types of scholarships are both for first-year and returning students. The majority of these scholarships are side wings to the full-ride program, and you may even qualify for both. Since you are not going to be paying for college, you have to get as many scholarships as you can. Even if you do get the "presidential" or full-ride scholarship, they are usually just enough to cover tuition and in some cases, room and board, but you will still need money to pay for your books and all the rest of your school supplies.

I also need to warn you that when you go to college, there will be a number of these "other" fees that you will have to pay, but usually these will be covered along with your tuition. These are fees like board tax, laundry fee, department fee, computer access fee, and identification card fee. Different schools have different charges, but it doesn't matter where you go, it never fails, and there will be some extra fees that you should incorporate in your financial plan.

Books are excellent resources. When I started out searching for scholarships, I believe it was at the end of my sophomore year of high school, but the only reason I started so early was because I was so curious and ready for college that I could not resist. There is so much information in books; all you have to do is pick one up and start reading. Now if you are like me, you may pick up a book, but not finish because you get sleepy or you just get out of the mood, but you have to force yourself to do it. I know you've heard this before, but the best way to get information is to sit back relax, pick up a book and read. Just like this book. Just think if you hadn't gotten this, you would have missed all of this information.

The first book I picked up when I started my search is called *The Scholarship Book.* This is a very thick book that is updated just about every year. They have so many scholarships in this book that you will start getting tired of looking. In the top right corner of the pages in the book are the main categories which are separated by major and there is a section entitled "General". In the general section, you will see scholarships in alphabetical order separated in a wide range of categories, including: state, background, organizations, trust funds, and more. Use these categories to help find out about scholarships that you qualify for. This will help you fine tune your search and it will be easy to find what you are searching for. For a lot of these scholarships, the book will only provide an address, sometimes a contact person's name, and maybe even a telephone number. A lot of those scholarship listings will also have Web sites.

When looking through the book, jot down information given on each scholarship for which you qualify. Don't try to just go through the whole book and remember what pages certain information was on, with plans to go back through later and take notes. Begin taking down information as soon as you find it. The book has so much information, you will end up forgetting where most of the scholarships you wanted were located. If the book supplies you with a phone number, call and ask them to mail you an application, and if you have a fax, try to get the information faxed, because that way you will get it faster. If they don't have a phone number, you have to write a letter. You can use the same letter for all scholarships you want to apply for. You just need a general business letter that asks them to mail you the scholarship application.

If the book doesn't give a name, make the letter out to: TO WHOM IT MAY CONCERN, or even better, SCHOLARSHIP COMMITTEE. Your letter doesn't have to be anything fancy; it can be something like this:

Date **(quadruple space)**

Your address
City, State, zip code **(quadruple space)**

Their name
Their address
City, State, zip **(double space)**

Scholarship Committee: **(double space)**

*I was searching through the (*Name of the Book*). I found your scholarship and I would like some more information on it. Please mail me an application package to the address above. Thank you for your time, and I look forward to receiving more information about your program.* **(double space)**

Sincerely, **(quadruple space)**

(Sign your name in this space)

Your Name (type your name here)

You can write something as simple as that and it will be sufficient. Remember, some of these companies are receiving hundreds of letters a day, and they don't really have time to read long, drawn-out letters, but there are others that will not have received letters from anyone but you. It is still polite to keep it simple because they will have enough time to find out all the other necessary information about you through your application. This will also help you save time; this way you don't have to spend a lot of time on each individual letter. You need to save as much of your energy and time for that application. All of this must be taken in account when you are drafting the letter. By all means, if you have a different letter that you would like to send, be my guest, as long as you indicate who you are, what you want, and how you can be reached. If you don't get an answer from them within two to three weeks, call them again or send another letter. There is no such thing as bugging them too much; in the business world, that is called persistence and guess what? It's a good quality to have. You should follow the same format as the letter above, but here is just an example of what a follow-up letter may look like:

Date **(quadruple space)**

Your address
City, State, zip **(quadruple space)**

Their name
Their address
City, State, zip **(double space)**

Scholarship Committee: **(double space)**

I mailed a letter to you a few weeks ago about your scholarship, but I haven't received a call or a letter from the company. I am hoping that my letter didn't get lost in the mail, but in the event that it did, I am providing my information again. **(double space)**

Sincerely **(quadruple space)**

(Your signature)

Your name typed

The Scholarship Book is not the only good resource for scholarships; there are all kinds of books that will help you find scholarships, and also magazines usually print a scholarship information edition once a year. You may even want to check out the newspaper. Remember, you are not going to pay for college, and since there are so many scholarship companies giving away money, you don't have to take time and do the research. Access as many books as you can possibly find. The time you spend is well worth it.

Just about every company that you can think of provides scholarships, and I do mean every. It's good to do for one reason: they are giving back to the community. It helps those who support them, and they can also write the "free money giveaways" off on their taxes at the end of the year, which is a plus for the company. Do not hesitate to bug the heck out of people to get a scholarship. At first they may view you as annoying, but after a couple of phone calls and a few visits, they will see what you really are: persistent, and persistence is what can take you a long way in any circumstance.

Some companies to get you started are: Target, they give out a scholarship every year, Walmart and Sam's Club both provide two one thousand dollars scholarships each year, you should check them out and any other stores that are like them. Pharmaceutical companies love to give out money; the scholarship is almost like an advertisement. The company believes that every time you tell someone you got a scholarship from Tylenol, for example, more people will be thinking about buying their products because they feel like "They're not such a bad company after all". Xerox, a lot of these big companies give out scholarships; they make so much money anyway, a thousand dollars here or there won't hurt their capital.

Other companies like that are: 3M and Motorola. Companies like Pepsico award students scholarships, and Kellogg's Cereals does too. I have not applied for scholarships from all of these companies, but we, ages between teens and twenties, are the main group that they advertise to, so if they don't give them out yet, they need to start. If they receive enough letters about a scholarship, even if they don't have a particular scholarship program now, I guarantee that it will go up for discussion in the next meeting and you will start hearing things about the "new program" they have just started. If enough people demand the same thing from a company, they will supply it because they would lose a lot of business if they don't. Never underestimate the power of numbers.

So if you are reading this book and you want to contact a company, but you're not sure if they give out scholarships, send them a letter anyway. I guarantee that there are many other students across the country sending that same company letters, and all they need is one more, yours, and it will go up for discussion. They won't be in the meeting saying, "All those in favor of providing a scholarship say aye." They will be saying, "We need to start providing students with scholarships, how much do you all think we should give?" You the students have just opened yourself another doorway to free education; take advantage of it and continue opening more doors.

If you think of a company that you want to send a letter to, but you can't find them in the phone book and you can't think of where to look, get on the Internet and look them up. Most companies have Web sites and they will usually look like this: We'll take Xerox for example, their website is *www.xerox.com.* Take that into consideration when you are searching. Once you find their Web site, there are going to be a lot of different places to go. You need to look for "Contact Us" or "Contact Information." This will either provide you with an e-mail or a physical address, maybe even a phone number. E-mail them, write them, call them and let them know you are interested in the scholarship they are offering. If they say they aren't offering a scholarship, you should inquire about their future plans for providing them. I want you to push forward with your search and I keep motivating you because you will have setbacks, but don't give up. There will be times that you feel all of your hard work is in vain, but don't give up. You may even get to the point where you start thinking, "I won't ever get a scholarship." That is not true; you will get many scholarships if you just don't give up.

We have covered colleges, books, and companies. Now it is time to dig deeply into something totally different from all of these: organizations. This country is filled with many organizations. There are fraternities (groups of men who share the same ideas and values), sororities (groups of women who share the same ideas and values), youth groups, religious organizations and others that abide in similar backgrounds, workplaces, or just habits. These organizations are different for the most part, but there are a few good similarities. One ideal that all of these organizations have in common is "Community Service," giving back to the community. It is through this section that they award students scholarships, locally and nationally.

People often apply for these scholarships, but there are a few myths about these organizations, at least the Greek ones, that need to be cleared up. Fraternities give scholarships to males and females, just as sororities. So if you are a young man and you have an idea what fraternity you want to join when you get to college, or a young woman who knows what sorority you want to be in, that is fine. Pursue that when you get there, but don't limit yourself to that one fraternity or sorority's scholarship. Apply for them all. Ladies, you should apply for all the fraternities' as well as all the sororities' scholarships. Guys, you should too. We will use Phi Beta Sigma Fraternity Incorporated for an example. If you would like to be a member of Phi Beta Sigma Fraternity, Inc. and you get a scholarship from Kappa Alpha Psi Fraternity, the brothers are not going to say, "He can't be in our organization because he got a scholarship from another frat," and they won't say that if you get a scholarship from a sorority either; so apply for everything that you come in contact with.

Just remember this: APPLY FOR EVERY SCHOLARSHIP THAT YOU GET. They won't award scholarships according to the applicant being a prospect for their organization. Students who are worthy of receiving the scholarship, males or females, can receive scholarships from fraternities or sororities.

A lot of churches give out scholarships to their youth just because they are graduating. Most of the time if it's a big church, the student members have to apply for it, but a lot of the small churches don't require that. They just give each student who is a graduate a certain amount of money. Depending on the church, there maybe an organization, board, or group, such as the choir, that may give out one scholarship to the most deserving graduate. You should know what types of things your church does in this event because you have been attending it for so long. If you don't know, ask somebody. As with companies, maybe your church does not give scholarships to graduates; you could be the member who starts that tradition. It's never too late to start giving out scholarships. If you talk to the Pastor, Preacher, Reverend, Father, depending on your denomination, you all can get this started. This does not apply just to Christians. No matter what religion you are, talk to the leader of your place of worship about a scholarship; either to apply for one or to start up a program. Take the initiative, and if you don't get any responses right away, be persistent until you do.

Every city has groups or organizations made up of people with commonalties. What I mean is, there are groups of people who share the same ideas, thoughts, business background, ethnicity, etc. and they give out scholarships too. Just to be clear, I'll give you an idea of what I am talking about. When I was little, my mother was a member of the National Association of Negro Business and Professional Women's Club (NANBPW). This organization was composed of a group of African American businesswomen and professional women. They did a lot of activities and also helped out the community in the best way possible. There are many other organizations just like this or with the same idea in your city. There was also an organization named Alpha Chi Boule, this was an organization of African American professional men, and they did the same types of things. Access these organizations and find out what types of scholarships they offer.

The two that I just named are just two examples. I'm sure there are groups of people who like computers, and organizations made up of teachers, elderly, or retired people. Find out what types of organizations your city has and get in touch with them. I'm positive they will be glad to guide you in the direction of their scholarship program, and they will also be happy to see that young people are interested in the things that they are doing.

There are three main ways to get information about organizations: talking to people, looking in the Yellow Pages, and checking through school files. The best way to get quick information is to talk to people, including your parents, teachers, counselors, parents' friends, co-workers, church members; all of these people can help you get information on scholarships. Ask about organizations that they are in and maybe organizations that they know other people are in. Find out what scholarships these organizations give, and what they are looking for in an applicant.

The most important thing you need to do is find out where and how you can get an application. The application is the key to their treasure and you need a key to get in. The second way to get information, when dealing with the organizations in your city, is to look in the phone book. The Yellow Pages were my best friend when I was looking for funding from local organizations. Go through the Yellow Pages and look for listings under "organizations," and "fraternal organizations," and you should find some good places to start.

The third and probably the easiest, is the file in your school. Just about all high schools have a file cabinet filled with scholarships from local and national companies and organizations. You can access this file at any time and get some applications for some of the places that are giving out scholarships. Collect all the scholarship applications that apply to you, but don't let this be your first and last stop. Continue looking and researching for scholarships in all of the other different avenues that I have explained and that you have thought of.

One of the best places to get scholarship information is the Internet. If you don't have access to the 'Net at home, I'm sure that your school has at least one computer with Internet access that you can use. While on the 'Net, there are two different ways that you can find scholarships, and both are very effective. One way is to access scholarship search Web sites. Two sites are *www.fastweb.com* and *www. studentadvantage.com.* Both of these sites and others just like them, require you to fill out some information about yourself.

Usually it takes about 15 to 20 minutes to finish, but I seriously advise you to fill them out carefully and truthfully. The only information that I wouldn't put on these sites is a credit card number. They should never ask you for one, and if they do, that means that they are trying to charge you for their service. Don't ever pay for this service, because for every one that charges you, there are three more that provide the same, if not better, service for free. The two I have indicated are free.

Now, if you just so happen to come in contact with a scholarship search site that asks for a credit card, before you completely get out of their site, scroll all the way down to the bottom of the page and see if there's a place that you can click that says "No Thanks." If there is, then click that and you can continue with your search for free. If it doesn't have the option to choose "No Thanks," then get out of that site and search for a free one. But make sure it doesn't before you exit the site. The reason is that you may have just run into some advertisement from another company that doesn't have anything to do with your scholarship search. A lot of times, you'll find that when you have access to something free, other companies place advertisements because they are the financial support of the site. It's sort of like an agreement they have. They say, "We will pay for your website so that your users can access your information free, as long as we can advertise our product or service on your site." You don't have to buy it and it's not going to help your search anymore if you decide to take the offer.

You also want to watch out for freebies. If you are filling out an application and it says, "Click here to win X amount of money," don't click there. It's just another advertisement, and you never win anything free. (Trust me, I've tried it) Just continue filling out the required information for your search. As I was saying, you have to fill in information about your background, like high school name, grades, test scores, organizations, leadership roles, college(s) you plan to attend, graduation date, parental information, and other items so that the database can narrow down their list to scholarship that apply to you.

There will be places where you can choose more than one item, in these cases hold down the "ctrl" button with one finger and click as many items that apply to you with the mouse. The site will usually have directions for what to do when choosing multiple choices; that is just a general way to do it. I highly recommend going through with the 15 to 20 minutes. A list of at least 30 scholarships that fit your background (educational, ethnic, and organizational) will come up. You can use this list to apply online, get applications e-mailed to you, or print out their address and mail them a letter as I indicated earlier. The searcher will usually e-mail you to inform you of new scholarships that have been added to your list or when a scholarship's deadline is getting close.

Along with Web sites that search for you, you can also go to search engines like *www.hotbot. com, www.yahoo.com,* or *www.mamma.com.* Once you get to these search engines you can either enter the type of scholarships you are searching for, like business scholarships, engineering scholarships, minority scholarships, or even organizations or companies that you want to search for. You can also search for sites that do the scholarship search for you. If you want to do that you should type in: scholarships, scholarship searchers, scholarship search engines, or anything to that effect. The Internet has all kinds of facilities within it, so you can optimize what you are searching for. Don't quit after using the search engines that I gave you. The 'Net, just like this world, changes every day. By the time this book comes out, some of these Web sites may not even be in use, so always try to keep yourself current with the best sites. You can find these in magazines, and by talking to people. Never let your search end at its beginning. I just want you to have somewhere to start you mind jogging. Usually the hardest part of doing research is trying to figure out where to start. I have helped and provided you with places to start; now all you have to do is continue.

Scholarships can be found just about anywhere. You just have to be willing to dedicate your time to do it. In actuality, it doesn't even take that long. Just spend at least two or three hours a week. Ten minutes here, fifteen there doing searches, talking to people, looking through books, and calling representatives. You will have a nice load of applications to fill out and since most scholarship applications don't have an application fee, you don't lose anything by filling them out.

I know that there are a million and one other things that you could be doing instead of looking for scholarships, and most of you are sitting there thinking that all of that other stuff is so important, you don't have time to do research on scholarships. But tell me truly: how many of those activities are going to actually help you in some way that is productive to you in the near or even far future? Even better, how many of these activities are going to make college free for you? You are paving the way for your life here and you should take it seriously.

Once you get into college and after you graduate, you will have to do research. Looking for scholarships is training for your personal researching skills. If you don't think you have any, here is a chance for you go gain some, and if you are already a fantastic researcher, you can put your skills to work, fine tune them and advance what you already know. Take the time to research your future. It Is worth It, mentally and financially. Like I stated earlier, I am just giving you the background and a foundation to get you started. I cannot stress this enough: don't stop at what I've offered as far as colleges, books, companies, organizations, and the Internet. Find other ways to get more information from your university. Look for more books than the Scholarship Book or "US News". Dive deeper into conversations with company representatives; talk to them until they give you the information that you are searching for. This is your future, not theirs. Access all the organizations in your town. Last, but definitely not least, when you get on the 'Net, try to find more and more Web sites that help people get scholarships.

Don't spend too much time on a Web site if it is not going to help you find scholarships. Move on to one that will, and then spend as much time as you need filling in information or even filling out applications; whatever the case may be, do it. Get those scholarships through hard work and determination.

III. Money That's Available

Well, I'm sure that you have realized by now that for the entire book, previous to this chapter, all that I have talked about is scholarships, scholarships, scholarships, and more scholarships. In actuality, except for this chapter, the book will be focused on scholarships for a lot of reasons. The main reasons are that scholarships, for one, are funds that you do not have to pay back **ever,** and for two, the amounts of money for scholarships, in most cases, exceed those of other funding sources.

But this book would not be a complete work unless I took the time out to present you with other ventures of funding. They are out there, but they are not all good and I will tell you why. When you finish reading this book, I want you to have an entire background on what to look forward to, how to approach different types of financial assistance, and what to look out for. You will be a financial guru by the time you are finished because you will not just know about funding, but you will understand the process, detail, and outlook of a successful college future.

As you know, the cost of education isn't cheap, but the value of education is worth a million times more than what you pay for it. You will not be able to pay for school if all you have to rely on is your job at a fast food joint. That's why I want you to know what your choices are. There are four main resources where students get money for college: personal funding, loans, grants, and scholarships. All of these are similar in that they are accessible to just about any student who goes to school. They all have certain restrictions that go along with them, but they are all different because the effect that each one has on your future is totally different. This chapter is going to focus on the different types of funding that you can get for your education and how each of them affects you.

I referred to the first section as "personal funding," but it's really money from your parents. There are a lot of young people who aren't fortunate enough to live with their parents, or they may get money from some other family member. So to make it easy, we will just say personal funding is money that comes from the direct bank account of someone close to you. Imagine this: you are in the summer before your first year of college, and from your research you found out that freshmen can have a car on campus. (Not all schools allow freshmen to drive cars.) You don't have a car yet, but for some reason you think your parents will get you one, since this is the first time in your life that you will be away from them for more than a month.

You start looking at inexpensive used cars with the idea that if you found a reliable car that wasn't too expensive, you could get it. Well you find it, a two-door Honda Accord, with eighty thousand miles on it. You ask your parents and guess what they say: "We really wanted to buy you a car, but since you didn't get any scholarships, we have to put all of our money towards your education. I'm sorry, but I guess you will just have to wait until you finish school or unless you make enough money this summer to buy it yourself."

It was in your hand, you had the car, you had the price, but you didn't have the most important thing: the money. We'll use the word "guardians" because it includes parents, grandparents, aunts, uncles, and any other person who takes care of you. Your guardians can only make so much money a year, and don't forget that they have to do certain things for themselves that are required: pay bills, buy groceries, and have a little fun too. Now they also have to pay for you. Do you really want to put that type of strain on someone? For the next four to five years, they have to look forward to paying four to fifteen thousand dollars out of pocket each semester. Now, that's twice a year for you mathematicians. Thirty thousand dollars a year is close to an average American citizen's household income. Even if they made sixty thousand a year, 50 percent of that is going towards school for you.

Do you know what I could do with thirty thousand dollars; Do you know what they could do? They would probably buy you the car gleefully because you just saved them from spending a hundred fifty thousand dollars over the next five years. I would buy you the car if I were them and some new speakers to put in the trunk. Some parents, I would even dare to say, the majority of all college students' parents, don't have thirty thousand dollars extra each year to even attempt to pay for their child's education. You have to think about stuff like this when you are sitting on your lazy butt on the couch in front of that television when you could be sitting at the table or desk, still watching television, but also filling out a scholarship application at the same time. This is serious business. You are not just affecting yourself anymore; other people are involved and you have to be cognizant of that.

Personal funding is limited, and it can limit you to future assets that you may want to acquire. Think about that. Is not taking the time to fill out a scholarship worth missing out on something you may want in the future: new clothes, shoes, A CAR? Even better, is sitting around thinking that you aren't good enough for a scholarship a valid reason for you not to take the time to find those applications, sit down and fill them out? I decided that the answer to both of those questions was NO, and you should too. Personal funding is usually the first and last place that students look for funding. Unless your parents are filthy rich, which is usually not the case, there is no reason you should have them spend any money on you for your education. I understand that they are there for you always, but now is the time to step up to the plate. You are almost grown. Get money for school on your own, and later you will truly have more pride in your education.

Once you get to school, you will be bombarded with all types of loan offers. They will have all different interest rates and other business jargon that make it seem like you are actually getting the better deal out of what they are talking about, but you should know, you never get the better deal! When it comes to loans, do what I do: JUST SAY NO. For the simple reason that I would like you to have a full understanding of what types of funds are available, I will take the time out to explain exactly what loans are about, what types are offered, and the type of payment plans they have. I do not want you to think that I am recommending them because I am not. The only reason that I am doing this is because it is good to have history on all of your choices, even the bad ones.

There are different types of loans. The most obvious differences are: regular loans and emergency loans. To get any type of loan you have to fill out a financial aid application. In most schools, this application is different from the scholarship application, so you don't necessarily have to fill this out, but check with your chosen school to make sure. After you've filled out your financial aid application, you will receive a statement that indicates what types of financial aid you can receive. Grants are included in this amount, but for the sake of this section, we will focus solely on loans. Now let's say for instance a student, (not you because you **will not** apply for loans), but let's just say a student gets a statement back indicating that they can receive seventeen thousand dollars worth of loans. I'll tell you what the majority of students do. They take this full amount of money and pay for school. For this scenario, we will just say that it costs ten thousand dollars for school. Now they have seven thousand dollars left; **SEVEN THOUSAND**.

First what happens is that they forget that this is a loan, and it must be paid back. And second, they start thinking about all the nice things they want to buy. You will see this yourself when you get on campus. Students will all of a sudden have all kinds of new clothes. Some may get a car (used, of course, because it's only seven thousand; that's not much when you are trying to get a brand new car), or jewelry, etc. They continue doing this each semester for five years until they graduate. Now don't forget, they have not received one bill for that loan yet. With loans for college, they usually don't begin charging for it until after graduation, but back to the story.

They receive seventeen thousand dollars for five years. That's two semesters' worth, thirty four thousand a year, one hundred seventy thousand dollars that they have received over that course of time. Even though they haven't started paying on it yet, interest has been and will continue to be accumulated to the loan. We will say it was a loan with a 20 percent interest rate. That takes that 170 that they received to two hundred four thousand dollars that they have to pay off the top. That means if they wanted to pay all of it off as soon as they got out of college, they would have to pay the loan company two hundred four thousand dollars. Now if they don't pay that much, depending on the time period that your rate is, (annually, bi-annually, quarterly, etc.) that loan would go up to three hundred thousand dollars within ten years after college. They will end up paying one hundred-thirty thousand more than what they received. Do you want this to be you? I didn't think so. It happens all the time because people don't realize what they are getting into, but this will happen no more, and you will not fall victim to this scam.

You do not want to be spending the rest of your life trying to pay off your loans. If it is not paid off in time, it will have accumulated so much interest that you will be. If I were to have to find something worse than having to use my personal money or even my parents' personal money to pay for college, I would have to say it would be worse to have used my personal money or my parents' money to try to pay back loans.

There was a time that I almost took out a loan. It was summer semester of 2000. I have a scholarship that is only good for four years, so inevitably I have to graduate within four years or all my money will be gone. At the end of that spring semester, I realized that the only way that I would be able to graduate within my four-year time frame was if I went to school that summer. To give you a better picture of the scenario, it was the beginning of May, two more weeks in between the end of the spring semester and the beginning of the summer semester; I told my mom that I needed a plane ticket, because I was going to go. She had no idea that I wasn't going to have enough money to pay for school and she surely didn't have any money. It was such short notice that I just didn't even bring it up.

I got to school and realized I had one week to figure out how I was going to pay for school. I decided if I had no other choice, I would just take out an emergency loan (the ones with the highest interest rates) and then just use that to pay for the summer, and since it was summer school it wasn't that expensive.

While I was sitting in class one day, one of my friends asks me where I was working for the summer. I told her that I was unemployed and about to get put out of school. She told me that one of our professors, who just so happened to be someone I had previously worked for, was hiring students to be tutors/mentors for this summer bridge engineering program. And she

59

said they were paying fairly well. Before class was even over, I walked out and went to talk to him about a summer job and he hired me. What my friend forgot to tell me was that not only would the job pay me an hourly wage, but it would also pay for my college tuition, room and board, and fees. When I found out that information, it was a day before I would have been kicked out. God saved me that summer and I have been thankful ever since. If it had not been for that job and the conversation with my friend, I would have never even thought to speak to my professor, and I would have never gotten a scholarship for that summer. That is why I say talk to people. They are the best resources for information. Not everybody is helpful, but it is usually the people that you don't think will be able to help you that have the best information.

Loans are bad; they are like thieves because you end up paying more on the interest than you actually got for the loan. That is ridiculous and that's why I tell everybody that I come in contact with to say no to loans. There are all kinds of loans: subsidized, non-subsidized, it does not matter. They are all bad because sooner or later, you will have to pay them back. The emergency loans like I almost had to take out are the worst because they know you have to have the money so the interest rates are sky high. When you are doing a search on the Internet or you fill out some paperwork for financial aid and it asks you if you want information on loans, what you going to say? *NO!*

Even when you say no, sometimes you will be approached with loan information or even be sent a loan application. Don't pay attention; act as if they aren't there, because they will bring you down and you don't want to be at home one day five years after you've finished college and get a bill in the mail about a loan. It's just not worth it.

Grants are the second-best mode of financing your education. They are great because it is money from the government that you receive, but don't have to pay back. Although they are good, along with them are many stipulations that must be looked over. Only certain people can get grants. I don't know the exact stipulations, but it has to do with how much money your parents make, if you were raised in a one parent home and some other details of your financial background. There is also an amount of money that you as a student can earn each semester that is affiliated with that and this amount is what makes getting grants bad.

Every semester, I try to get enough scholarships so that I will get an overbalance and get some money back. One particular semester I had an overpayment of about two thousand dollars. I was so excited about getting the money that I began to get greedy. I started thinking, "I know there's a way that I can get more than just two thousand dollars." So I went to the financial aid office and had them look up my information.

The lady at the desk said, "You know that you are eligible to receive fifteen hundred dollars from a Pell Grant that you were awarded." I told her that I didn't want it because I wasn't sure what grants were. I did a little research and found out that they were almost like scholarships because if I got it, I wouldn't have to ever pay it back. Then the greed kicked in again. Voices in my head started saying, "Man, get that money, that's fifteen hundred dollars more you can have. You will be walking around campus with thirty five hundred dollars!" A few days later, I went back to the Financial

Aid Department and told the lady I decided to accept the grant and she went ahead and put it on my fees.

I waited a week to go to the Fiscal Office, that's where they hand out the checks, because it usually takes that long for extra money to kick in so that they can write another check. To my surprise, when I got there to check my balance, the clerk told me that my balance was at zero dollars and zero cents. I said, "How could that be, just last week I had an overbalance of two thousand dollars, and I just got Pell Grant?"

She said, "I don't know, but you may want to go check with the Financial Aid Department because they will have the details on your account."

I went back to that same person who was smiling in my face telling me that I could have all this extra money, with a pissed off attitude and started fussing and complaining about what happened. Instead of fixing the problem, she sent me to my financial aid counselor. My counselor informed me that along with grants and other aid, not including outside scholarships, there is a certain amount that the university is allowed to give each student. Each student has a different amount, but all students who apply for aid have this barrier. I was told that upon receiving my Pell Grant, I overstepped my barrier and they have to reduce my scholarship from the university to compensate for my grant. They didn't take the grant, but they subtracted just enough from my other scholarship that the university gave me to bring my balance to zero. I didn't think that they could do it, but they justified their actions by saying scholarships by the university are not to be used to support overpayments.

That's why I say watch out for grants. If I hadn't been greedy and tried to get that grant, they would not have worried about the amount of money that I was receiving and I would have had two thousand dollars to go in my pocket, but because of greed, I lost it all. Take this into consideration when you are thinking about accepting your grants. You should check to see how much it is, but don't take it out unless you absolutely have to.

The essence of a scholarship is so enticing because you don't have to pay it back EVER. Doesn't that sound amazing? It's almost like free money. Only it's not free because you have to work for it. The only way you should pay it back is by passing information to others about higher education, scholarships, and other helpful information for the future, just as I am doing for you. You don't necessarily need to write a book, but you have other ways of informing people about it. Referring someone to this book is an option in itself. Just make sure that you tell somebody how to prepare for the future.

I also like scholarships so much because they require you to sit down and think for a little while. You have to think about the personal information and what you plan on putting in your essay. No matter what the case, you will always have to put some effort into it. This effort is what adds value to the work that you are doing. Say for example one day you come home and your parents have bought you a brand new car. (I use the car example a lot.) You will drive that car carelessly, and if you get into an accident in that car, it won't matter because deep inside you're thinking, "Oh well, they'll just have to buy me a new car". You have placed no value on this vehicle and therefore treat it like junk.

63

Now say for instance your parents say, "If you earn at least a 3.6 GPA each marking period of this year, we will buy you a brand new car." Two things will happen: one, you are going to work hard to make sure that you get that 3.6 every time so that when June comes around, you can be riding around in a new car, and two, when you drive that car, you are going to drive it carefully. If it's a sports car you may drive fast, but still, you'll drive carefully. You are going to make sure that you don't wreck the car because you don't have a clue if they will buy you another one. You hold special value on it because you have worked for it. You earned it. You take pride in it. That is the same way you will feel once you receive that letter in the mail saying that you are one of the recipients for this year's scholarship. Even if you have an overpayment from your scholarships, you won't waste it away because you had to work hard for it. You don't get that same feeling or put that same value on the other sources because you don't have to put forth that much effort toward receiving them.

Scholarships are split into many different categories, but there are two categories that you need to pay special attention to: one, where the funding originates, and two, how the funding is allocated. The first category has to do with overpayments. Once you get into school, you will notice that you have received scholarships that are university scholarships and "outside" university scholarships. University scholarships are usually your full rides, presidential, half ride, honors scholarships. These are directly from the university that you plan to attend. You need to pay special attention to these because they have stipulations that go along with them. With most, there is a certain GPA that you must attain each semester to keep the scholarship, and if you ever fall into the situation where you can get an overpayment, the university can reduce the amount they are signed to give you because of the "we don't support overpayments" statement that they gave me.

The other types are scholarships that you received that aren't affiliated with the school. What makes these scholarships so great is that the university can't hold back any money that you receive in case you get an overpayment. They are required to give you back the money that you have extra. So, if you have a ten thousand dollar overpayment from outside scholarships, you don't have to worry, you will be sticking a ten thousand dollar check in your pocket soon.

The second category that I stated deals with the time frame that you receive that money. This is particularly important because it helps you plan your future. Some scholarships are automatically renewable; usually under the circumstance that you retain the GPA they require you to get it each semester. Whatever the case may be, there is always a time stipulation on a scholarship. Usually the university scholarships are set to continue as long as you are in school. My presidential scholarship, in particular, is set for eight semesters. It doesn't matter if I graduate or not, but after eight semesters within the time frame of four years, my scholarship ends.

There are some scholarships that are only offered for one semester. Some are for one year. With a few scholarships, you can just fill out a renewal for the next term and automatically get the scholarship again for the same duration of time. Usually when you receive it, and actually a lot of times when you get the application, you can find out the duration of the scholarship and the possibility of automatically renewing it. Just do your research and you will find out. But for a general outlook, most scholarships that are one thousand dollars or less are usually for one semester and you have to fully reapply to get them again. Scholarships that are more than one thousand are usually split up between two semesters and usually have a renewal form. Mostly all full ride scholarships are automatically renewable until you graduate.

In all cases, there are exceptions, so if you don't see it on the scholarship application and it isn't indicated on the award letter when you get the scholarship, call the phone number on the letter and ask someone. Find out if it's renewable and if so the process for renewing, and then you will be set. You will, on the other hand, run into one-time scholarships of all amounts, and even if it is a one-time--one semester/one year, whatever the case may be--still reapply for the scholarship the next year. They will remember you as a previous recipient and this will increase your chances of receiving the award.

Once you get in school, you will also come across something that is very tempting. It will be offered with all kinds of gifts and fun opportunities. You will get so many T-shirts, pens, and pencils from these places; you will think that you are going crazy. I was so shocked at these companies. I would sit there and try to figure out why they were offering their products to me, when I see all kinds of commercials on TV about grown folks who can't get them.

I am talking about credit cards. I'm telling you, so many folks will come at you with this stuff that it will make you want to put a fake name on their list just so they will give you their stuff and leave you alone. It is crazy. Don't fall in their traps because, just like loans, they are traps. But, unlike loans, what will happen is that you get all these credit cards, go out and buy some stuff, and they start charging you right away. If you don't pay them, it will make your credit bad. This really affects you in the future because with bad credit you will find that it is hard to get financed for a car and even a house, and you don't want that.

But the flip side to that coin is that if you don't get any and you never have to make payments, when you try to get financed for that car, you still won't be able to get it because you won't have any credit at all. Or, if they do finance you, you will have some tremendous rates. I recommend that you get one credit card; ONLY ONE. Only use this when you have to, and I don't mean like, "Oh, I just have to buy those new shoes". No, the only time I use my credit card is when I have enough money in the bank to cover it, and they say they only accept credit cards for payment. For instance, when I buy plane tickets, I use my credit card. It comes in handy and I make steady payments on it. Even if you want to get a cell phone, if you have enough money to get it, get it, and you can use your credit card to pay for it. As you are making payments on your credit card, you are also building up your credit. It is good when you use your credit card for things like that, but you have to be careful. When you have a credit card in your possession, it is like you have the whole world as opportunity to buy. You can go anywhere and buy just about anything you want with that card. It is almost like you have the power to do anything. When you have the card in your possession, it is almost like you completely forget that you are going to have to pay it back one day. When that bill comes, it is going to be just as bad as that loan. Credit cards have those same crazy interest rates. The only real difference between a credit card and a school loan is that you have to start paying on your credit cards the month after you have charged it. It really does not matter if you are in school or if you have been out of school for ten years. When you don't pay on those credit cards in the right amount of time, they start charging you even crazier late fees. So like I said earlier, watch out for stuff like that.

Well let's see, we have talked about all types of funding: personal funding, loans, grants, and scholarships. Now you should know exactly what types of funds are available to you. Watch out for the scams and become educated in all the possibilities of college funding.

IV. Applying Techniques

Getting the application is just phase one of your process. I understand that it may have been tough. Hopefully you are sitting down reading this chapter with at least 15 scholarship applications in your hand-- at least. If you don't have at least 15 applications, you need to stop reading right now, go back out and do some more research so that you can have at least, the very least, 15 applications. Now let me tell you why.

It is an honest fact that you will not get each and every scholarship that you apply for. There is no way around it; you will not get all of them. I am not saying that it is impossible, so just to stay politically correct, we shall just say that your chances of getting each and every one of the scholarships that you currently have in your possession is very low. Now you ask why. Well the reason is, there is a student somewhere in this country, at this moment, right now, who has the exact same credentials as you do. They will not be applying for all the same scholarships that you are applying for, but let's just say you have only three applications in your hand right now, and they just so happen to have one of them, and both of you send them out early and the scholarship board reviews both of them. Now, they have to decide between that other person and you. I cannot say for sure which one of you the scholarship board will choose because you both have the same grades, test scores, and we'll even say you both have the same amount of officer roles (I'll cover these later). One thing that I can tell you is that your chances of getting a scholarship is five times better when you have fifteen applications than if you have three.

The truth of the matter is that you probably won't have someone with the same exact credentials as you on all of the scholarships, but they will be pretty close. That's why I say that you should apply for as many scholarships as you possibly can because you want to receive the maximum amount of scholarships. Fifteen is a low number, but it is a start, and that's what you should set your foundation at.

I don't know if you have realized it or not, but most of this is about setting a foundation. Goals are good and they need to be reached. Your goal is to go to school for free, and if possible, earn enough scholarships that you get some of it back in the form of an overpayment. In order to do that, you have to set foundations, and then build off those foundations until you have finally reached your goal. When you reach your goal, you will then look back and see all of the knowledge you have acquired, the types of things you have learned, and values you have gained. That will make this whole process worth it so much more.

I promise when you finish with all this, you will think, "I never imagined all that time I thought I was wasting would result in this. I never thought that I would get more out of filling out a scholarship application than just scholarship money." The money is good, but along with the money, you will gain so much more that the money will become ten percent of the value of how you feel about yourself. You may not believe me right now; I won't lie, when I was where you are right now, I never would have imagined that I would say stuff like that to myself, but I did and so will you, once you have achieved this goal.

The application itself is just a collection of papers with blank spaces on it. You won't be just filling it out, you will be giving it life, and this life is what represents you. Do not leave anything out. I don't care what it is, no matter how small you think what you have done is; it may be what puts you over the top and gets you the scholarship. What in the heck am I talking about? I am talking about what you put on the application when you're applying for a scholarship. I will explain.

A scholarship application can range anywhere from one page to fifteen pages. Sometimes the number of pages is related to how much money they are offering. Do not pass on a one-page scholarship just because they are not giving a lot of money, and most definitely do not pass on a ten- to fifteen-page application because you don't feel like spending all the time needed to finish it. You need to approach each and every scholarship the same exact way, and what's the big deal? You are basically filling in the same exact information. Maybe a little more here and a little less there, but it is all from the same foundation, which is you. All applications, no matter how big or small, will have these four sections:

1. Personal Information Sheet (P.I.S.)
2. Letters of Recommendation (L.O.R.)
3. Transcript
4. Essay

Each and every scholarship will require that you address each of these four topics. You can do it; they are not difficult at all, and they all help you out in the long run. Each section is separate and they all require a different type of effort. By the end of this chapter, you will know what each of these is, how to address them, and last but not least, how to come out on top.

The first section, P.I.S., is nothing more than the personal information sheet(s). This is the actual application. You should fill this out with all the knowledge that you have about yourself and try to be as current as possible. What types of things are you asked on the P.I.S? The P.I.S. basically just asks for you background information. In the part one of this section, you usually indicate things like: name, address, phone number, age, brothers/sisters, etc. This is just to give them a little knowledge about your background. This is plain, you know what it is, you know all the answers, and you are not required to think at all here. Just fill everything out honestly and move on to the next section.

The part two of P.I.S. is a little more in-depth. Usually this is the high school background section.

Now if you are looking at your application and the second section is not asking about your high school background, it is OK, just go to the section that does. This is where it gets tricky and also where a lot of students begin to leave stuff out that they don't think is worth including. Remember when I said to list all the officer roles that you have had? I was talking about this section. Under the high school information section, you have to put your GPA, and test scores, but also your program and organizational participation. Contrary to popular belief, everything that you have been involved in *does* count. You need to put all of it. If you were in the church choir, put it. If you were a Boy Scout, put it. If you were in student government, put it.

Do you understand what I am trying to say? Put each and every organization on the application, and when I said, "officer roles," I was talking about if you were the president, vice-president, secretary, treasurer, historian, representative, section leader (for those in band), youth group leader, etc. Whatever role you had in an organization, put it. You may have been the person who took pictures at all the events. Don't think for a minute that that is not an important role. You were the historian; you kept pictures of past events. That counts.

If you did not have an officer role, don't lie and make one up. Instead of doing that, just indicate that you were a member of that organization. You have to be honest on this application because if you are not, you will not put yourself in danger of not receiving that scholarship. I don't care what organization it was. THEY ARE ALL IMPORTANT, so put them all on the applications.

Many students feel like the only thing they should write down are the organizations at school that had membership in, but this is a myth. I'm glad you know now because you will not make that same mistake that they did. Many students participate in programs outside of school, and these same students omit these programs from their applications too. Do not do this. I know some of you are sitting there thinking, what is he talking about? Programs, what kind of programs do you mean?

Well let's see, when I was in high school, there were a number of programs I participated in. One of them was called the Michigan State University Mathematics and Science Program. It lasted the whole summer and we took classes, I mean real classes, and did a lot of activities throughout the program. I used some of the stuff that I learned that summer in high school for the next two years. On my applications where I was allowed to indicate programs I participated in, I wrote this one down. I also put down other programs that I was in, like King Chavez Parks College Day Programs (KCP). This is a pre-college program that gives minorities the opportunity to see what college life is all about. That program was actually a year-round program.

So, whether you were in something like Kids' College or Gifted/Talented, if you had the opportunity to take college classes while you were still in high school, no matter what you were a part of, put that down. They like to see that the person they are supporting is not only intelligent, but also outgoing. Writing down all your programs and organizations will exemplify that.

Right now, I want you to take a moment and think about all of the programs and organizations you have participated in from eighth grade until now. As you read these words, take out a piece of paper and write down everything that comes to mind: organizations, programs, leadership roles, and officer roles. Now, before you continue reading another word, stop reading and finish your list. When you have finished writing all that you can think of, start reading again.

Now I hope you wrote that on a nice, clean sheet of paper. If you didn't, stop reading again, get up, go find a nice, clean sheet of paper, and NEATLY write everything on that sheet. Keep this somewhere that you will remember to find it later, because you will need it. Now that you have your list, you are set. All of the applications that you fill out will include the same information on this list. I know a lot of you just continued reading and didn't even think twice about writing out your list, and if this is you, stop right now and do it. I keep stressing this because right now your mind is jogged and you are thinking about the organizations and officer roles. If you don't do it now, you may forget a lot of them later when the time comes to fill in your application. I recommend doing this because it's the same information; this way, when you get your application, you will not have to waste any time thinking of this information because it's already written down. You can just copy this sheet. Which will reduce time spent on each application.

There is no way to get around lying; that's why I say put your true information, true GPA, and true test scores. The truth always comes out in the light and you always will reap what you sow. It's better to put in quality work early in school so that when it comes time to fill out these applications, you will have been involved in many organizations, you have gotten good grades, and you have done well on the ACT and SAT tests. If you have not reached what I said to strive for, that's OK, you still have a good chance of getting the scholarship.

The second section of applying for a scholarship is letters of recommendation. This is one of the **most** important sections of your application. You may not see why, but it is personal accounts of information about you that a board will review. Think about it.

A board may have five thousand applications to review. All of the applicants have just about the same information on their application. They have indicated their background information, educational information, and parental information. All this is fine and dandy, but the board has no way of getting to know a person from mere statistics. Basically, that's what all the information on the P.I.S. is--just some statistical information about you indicating what you did and where you live, in case you are awarded the scholarship.

But the letters of recommendation are letters written by people who actually know you, adults who have had conversations with you, been in situations with you. They know what type of person you are. Are you a hard worker? Are you lazy? Are you a person who takes initiative? Or are you one who just follows the crowd? Are you a people person? Are you shy? Do you actively participate in class? Or do you just scribble and doodle on paper while in class? These letters of recommendation are ways to find out that type of information. That is why you need to get very good letters.

There are key people that you need to get a letter of recommendation from. Most adults are actually quite nice when it comes to recommendations. I know you probably have at least one teacher that you swear hates you. Every time you are in class, they always bother you or act like you're nothing. Usually this is the main teacher who wants to write you a letter. You will be surprised--they will most likely be the one who gives you the best of all your letters, so don't count them out. Like I said earlier, there are key people that you should ask to write you a letter of recommendation. But you need to develop a relationship with these people before asking them to write one. You need to get them to notice you IN A GOOD WAY. Be professional, say hi to them. Engage in conversations with them as often as you get a chance. Tell them the types of positive things you have been doing. This is their opportunity to get some background information about you, so when it comes time to write the letters they will be able to.

Now I'm sure you all know what "sucking up" or "brown nosing" means. Let me explain, this is when you go out of your way to impress someone. Say, for example, you see a teacher who was drinking coffee and their cup is empty. Asking them if they want you to fill it up, or even worse taking the cup from them and filling it up without even asking are both sucking up. This will not score any points with anyone. Actually it will make them look at you as if you are not being pure and true. So do not ever do that. Just be yourself. Do what feels comfortable to you. The essence of it is that you want them to see your true self, so that when they finally do write that letter of recommendation, the scholarship committee will be able to see your true self too.

You need to start talking to them as soon as possible. Your freshman year is the perfect time to start. Don't wait, because you want them to be able to indicate that they have known you for some years, and by the time you start filling out applications, your twelfth grade year, they will be able to say they have known you for three to four years, and this is perfect. Another thing that I notice people do that is bad is, they will start talking to the person freshman year and then not say another word to them until it is time for the recommendation. This is bad too because, for one, they have probably forgotten who you are, and for two, they won't have any comments to say about you that are recent. How does this sound?

"...I met Charles Phillips three years ago when he was a freshman. He was such a good student, he had good grades, and seemed to be participating in a number of programs. I'm sure he's been doing a great job since, and he will be an excellent candidate for the scholarship."

That would not be the whole letter, obviously, but even if that excerpt were in the letter, it would mess up the whole recommendation. If I were on a board, I would think this student might receive our scholarship and not bother to ever speak to us or thank us in the future, and this is bad. He or she would not be a good candidate.

Make sure you meet them your freshman year and try to keep as up-to-date with them as you can. It could be worth millions in your future. If you are reading this book right now and you are already past your freshman year, go introduce yourself tomorrow to anyone I indicate in this next paragraph. If you are at school right now, start talking to them now; you will have time to finish the book later. After you meet these folks, you can come back to it, and while you are reading, you will be giving them a chance to think what a wonderful student you are.

Now that I have covered what not to do and what to do, let me tell you whom to target. First, your principal; it is always good to have the person who is at the top of the pyramid recommending you. Think about it--if you were working at a company and you were working directly under a supervisor, and the CEO--who is the top of the chain--recommended you for a raise, don't you think that is better than just another supervisor recommending you? It most definitely is. The supervisor's recommendation would be good, but the CEO has a lot more pull.

That brings me to the next person, those whom you work directly under: your teachers. All of your teachers are excellent people to get letters from, but there are key teachers that you want. You need a letter from your most recent mathematics teacher, science teacher, and English teacher. Also, you need to get a letter of recommendation from someone who may or may not work in your school, but who does have a Ph.D. Now I know that you are reading this with one question in your mind: why? The majority of scholarship applications that you will fill out indicate that you will need three letters of recommendation: usually two letters from teachers and one from an outside source.

Some applications will ask that you have a specific teacher write you a letter of recommendation. If a certain teacher is specified, one that they are either going to ask for will be a mathematics teacher, science teacher (they may specify which science course), or an English teacher, guaranteed. With scholarship applications that do not ask for a specific teacher, it really doesn't matter, but why get other letters when you already have some?

Now, why should you get a letter from someone who has a Ph.D.? To a scholarship committee, a letter of recommendation from someone with a Ph.D. says more. People tend to follow in the footsteps of those they are around and look up to. If they see that you are recommended by someone with that level of education, it says to them that you will not be a failure, and that you will strive hard to achieve the same success as the person with a Ph.D. It weighs heavier than someone without it.

You have to remember, the people who are reading these letters don't know the people who are writing them personally; all they know is what they see: the occupation of the person, if they are your teacher or principal, or their educational status, if they are a Ph.D. or not. If you do not know anyone with a Ph.D., ask your parents if they know someone. It is probably someone you already know and you just never realized that they had one.

Ask all of the people that have written you a letter of recommendation to give you an unsigned copy of the letter. If they ask why, explain that you want to keep it in your files so that in case another scholarship arises in the next week or so, you can just make a copy of the letter and have them sign it, to prevent them from having to go through the trouble of printing it again or rewrite it altogether. This will reduce so much time in their schedule, and I promise you, they will thank you later. Do this with everyone you get a letter of recommendation from and make a folder called "LETTERS OF RECOMMENDATION." Before you send off any of these letters, read them. Make sure that what is said is something you agree with.

What if you read a letter and you don't like what it says? There are only two things that you can do in this case. One, send it with your scholarship application, or two, don't send it. If the letter you do not like is from a teacher that the application specifies they must get a letter from, you can ask another teacher that you had in a previous year who teaches the same subject (i.e. mathematics, English, etc.) to write you a letter of recommendation, but if you haven't taken any other teachers for that subject, you have to send the one you don't like. Just do not use it in any of your other applications that do not specifically ask for that teacher. It is good to have a variety of letters, because there will be applications that do not ask for any specific teacher or person for the letter, and you will have a choice of which letters to send. This is perfect for you, because you get to analyze all of your letters and then choose which ones you think are the best and mail them. Do not in any case, ever go to a person who wrote you the letter and ask them to rewrite it. That is rude and they will observe you as an ungrateful person. That is like burning a bridge, and you never want to do that.

Make sure that you get your letters before you start filling out your applications; this way you won't have to wait for your teacher to write you one. It would be ideal to get your letters early in the fall semester, and you want them to be current with your application. You want the date on the recommendation to be within two weeks of the date that is on your application, where you have signed. So this is what you should do: Instead of having them write your letters in August or September, go to them and ask them if they will be willing to write you a letter, and that you will get back to them on the day you need it. This way they will be able to think about what they want to say about you. When you first get your scholarship application, go back to them and ask them if they can have it ready for you in a week. This keeps you within that two-week frame of currency, and you can also send more than one scholarship application at once. If you have ten scholarship applications and you read the letter and like it, you can have them sign ten copies at once and send them off together. You may think it is asking too much or being overbearing, but it is not. Actually that shows ambition and pursuance. Both are true values needed for achieving goals.

The third section of the application is the transcript. The transcript is an official document that you cannot change. Everything that is on your transcript is written in stone and will continue to be that way. You cannot alter it and the only things that will change on it are your cumulative grade point average and class rank, which is solely based on what you do in your classes. You always want to get the most recent transcript, because it will show the progress that you have made in school. This is why you need to do the best you can in all your classes. If you lie on the application about your grades, it will be reflected and found out when the board reviews your transcript. You cannot hide this. There is not one scholarship that I have applied for that did not ask for my transcript. They all ask for it.

Your transcript is a record of all the grades that you have earned in school. They are only calculated on a semester basis, so don't worry about it if you do not do so well on a certain marking period. But if you mess up an entire semester, it will be reflected and will not be able to be taken back, so try your hardest to get good grades. You should aim for at least a 3.7 grade point average (GPA). A four point is the perfect grade, but that leaves no room for error, and a three point seven allows you to have messed up in one or two courses, but also challenges you to bring up those mess ups; so aim for that.

Do not aim for anything lower than a three point seven, but I do challenge that you aim for a GPA higher than that. Always maintain your GPA, don't forget, it doesn't matter if you got an A because of extra credit or if you got an F because you missed one test. When the scholarship review board looks at your transcript, they will not see the reason why you got a letter grade, they will just see that you got it. If they see an A, they are going to think that you worked very hard in that class, you were an active participant, and you did well on your assignments. If they see an F, they will think you were lazy, you didn't care too much about the class or your grade for that matter, you hardly ever participated, and basically they would be wasting their money on you if they gave you the scholarship.

Your grades are a reflection of you. Even though they don't fully explain what you did that semester, it is all they will have to go on. If you do well, they will embrace you and you will have nothing to worry about.

I love the last section of the application. It is my most favorite and least favorite all in one. This is the section that will stop some people from even applying for the scholarship. Do not be one of those people. I do not care if the scholarship asks for 10 words or if they ask for ten thousand words; write them. You are always a winner when you write your essay. The main reason is that it keeps your mind jogged and you are forced to practice your writing skills. I did so well in my English class the semester I was writing all those essays because it kept me up-to-date.

When you are typing your essay, keep in mind what the topic is. All scholarship applications will have some type of topic for the essay. You need to keep this topic in your mind and write your essay around it, because if you do not, you will not get the scholarship. If I were on the scholarship board and I read an essay from one of the prospective applicants, and their essay didn't have anything to do with our scholarship topic, there is no way I would let them get the scholarship. That applicant is showing me that they cannot follow directions, or maintain a focused mind enough to write a quality paper on what was asked.

Let's get away from the dreary part of the essay. This should be your favorite part. It's the essay! This is your time to shine. When they read this they will get a personal view of you. This is somewhat like your letters of recommendation, only the letters give them a second person view. Someone is talking about you and the board gets to see how others view you. But the essay gives the scholarship board something more than a second person view. It puts them in your mind. It shows your mental capacity and your everyday thinking. These essays are usually about your opinion: What do you want to do when you get older? What are you going to major in and why? Who most influenced you and why?

These are not hard questions. You can spend hours and hours writing about these topics because they are things that you know so well. All you have to do is write about a hundred words on this topic, whereas in reality, you could write a million. So when they ask you one of those questions, just start writing. Write, write, and write until you don't think you can write anymore. Put it down for a couple of hours, let your mind jog, then come back to it and write some more. Just keep writing on the topic until you absolutely, positively have no more words in your exhausted mind to flush out on paper, and then edit it.

The first stage of editing is to find out how many words you have written. This is the easy part, because all you have to do is go to the "word count" on whatever software program you are using, and it will tally the number of words you have typed. You can balance what you do next by how many words you have and how many words you need. If you have more words than they ask for, then you need to take some stuff out. There is a reason that they asked for that specific number of words, if you go over that, you will probably not get the scholarship. The only exception is if the scholarship says, "Please write at least X number of words." If it says "at least," then you will be OK to type more than they ask for, but if you see the words "at most" or "no more than" or "maximum" you know that if you go over you will be disqualified, and you do not want that to happen. It will be a waste of everything that you have done and everyone who helped you (including those who wrote your letters of recommendation).

If you do not have enough words, you need to first go through with your spell checker, (actually you should do this in all occasions); after you have done that, you need to use my techniques to add words. Where ever you have "can't, could've, it's, I'm…" any words like that, separate them. So instead use "can not, could have, it is, I am…"; those are little cheats, but they work. This way you aren't changing your essay too much and the point that you are trying to get across will still come.

If you have too many words, do the opposite. Instead of saying "should have" say "should've," and all the other situations in your essay you can find like that. If that still does not give you the number of words that you are striving for, you may need to reevaluate your sentences. There are always at least two ways to say the same thing. There is a short way and there is a long way. If you need more words, go to all of your sentences where you have expressed something the short way, and try to think of a longer way to say it. I promise after doing this throughout your entire essay you will find ways to re-state sentences and you will also have other ideas in your head to optimize your essay and you will have what you are searching for: a very well thought out explanation of what you were trying to say in the amount of words that the board has set.

This chapter is one of the most important of this book. I hope you have detailed and reread each and every line of it so that you know it like the back of your hand. Filling out the application and taking your time to think about what you are going to write in your essay are very important. A lot of students crash their opportunity to get their education for free because they lack the value of time. You have to value the extra time that you have in a day and use that "free time" to get scholarships. Even if you do have the money or somebody tells you that they will take care of your college education's finances, you should still try to get scholarships because then you can use that other money to get yourself something else.

What have we discussed in this chapter? You now know what the P.I.S. and L.O.R. are (my personal acronyms), what each section of the application involves, how important the transcript is, and what types of detail needs to be in your essay. You are now ready to fill out your scholarship application. This is what you have worked for. This is your time to shine. I cannot get you the money; only you can do that. I can show you the right path to take, and set you on your journey, but <u>you</u> personally have to take the footsteps to fulfill your destiny.

Just imagine, all of these scholarship applications that you are filling out are going to transition into real cash money. I don't think you understand exactly what this means. You are spending an hour or two making yourself five hundred to ten thousand dollars, maybe even more. You are about to be paid! But don't stop at just one or two scholarship applications. Apply for as many as you can. The more you apply for, the more your chances of getting top dollars. I want you to keep this in mind, every time you hear about a scholarship or see an application. I don't care if it is as thick as a novel or as tiny as a quarter of a sheet of paper. Find out where you can get an application, go pick up the application, and fill it out as if you were already signing the acceptance letter for the money. You will be signing that letter and you will be getting that money, but first you have to put some hard work into it. You have to want it. You have to work for it. You have to earn it.

V. Last Years of High School

These are your last days of high school. Can you believe it? In a year or two, you are finally going to be in college! A lot of things are going to happen between now and then. I know you are looking forward to getting out of high school and starting college, but don't forget that there are some good times still left in high school. The worst thing a person can do is spend so much time looking forward to what is going to happen, that they forget to treasure and hold onto all that is happening right now. Right now, you are at the top of the pyramid: juniors and seniors. Everybody looks up to you. As you walk down the halls, all the freshmen and sophomores say, "Wow, I can't wait until I am finally in their shoes. The upperclassmen at our school are just so cool. They look good and they have good grades." You are the role models for the freshmen and sophomores.

Don't spend so much time preparing for college that you lose your high school pride. Use some of your time giving back to them. You have to be nice because, just think, when you step on that campus, you are really going to want all those upperclassmen to be nice to you. If not, you will never find where any of your classes are, where the parties are, what professors to take, and on and on and on. Along with learning how to get scholarships, I also want you to develop the value of giving back, because it is very much needed. You should always want to give back to those who are under you, because when you were in their place, someone gave to you. Someone helped you get to where you are today.

What is going to happen in these last two years? So much is going to occur during your last two years of school, you almost forget the most important thing: education. First, you are going to get all kinds of mail. I don't know if you usually get a lot of mail, but it doesn't matter, because for the last two years of high school, you are going to get mail like crazy. I know you think that I am joking, but I am serious when I say one day you are going to come home from school and see that your mailbox is overflowing with mail, and all of it is going to be for you. Your parents may get mad because they have been waiting for something for the last couple of weeks, but you might as well tell them to just let you go through the mail every day, because you are going to have to filter out this stuff anyway.

The mail I am talking about is college information. You are going to get all kinds of pamphlets, letters, applications, and all of this stuff is just advertisements. That is it. These universities know that if you come to their school, you are going to help their statistics because you are a success-oriented person. They want you in their school so that they can put your high test scores on their statistics for the next group of students. It is also just to inform you about different universities. It is always so much better for a person to have options.

There will be a lot of schools that you recognize. You may even get lucky enough to get a letter from the "school of your dreams," that one school you have been dying to go to. For the most part, though, you will receive mail from universities and colleges that you have never heard of. I am not kidding. I mean schools with some obscure names, and you will start thinking to yourself, "This isn't a real school, is it?"

You will want to throw away most of that stuff. I am not going to tell you that you should throw that information away or that you should not. That is up to your discretion. Some of the information will be very enlightening and actually good for you to read because they give background on schools. This is good for people who are not sure where they want to go, because then you can go through the packages and find out about schools from everywhere.

Among other things, you can find out what types of majors the school offers, the type of climate they have, how many students the university has as a whole, and the number of students per class there will be. Some of the bigger universities have classes with five hundred students in them and then there are other schools that only have 10 to 20. You can use all of this information to help you decide.

The one thing that I really hated about getting those letters is that hardly any of the packages that I received had an application for a scholarship in them. Half of them did not even have an application for admission. I could not believe that they didn't have a scholarship application. In my mind, if a school really wanted to get me, they would at least provide me the opportunity to get one of the scholarships they were offering. If this happens to you, do not be discouraged. Many times schools will not send that type of information because they only want to give it to students who are planning to come to their school. It's good to check out some of the information just so you can get a feel for it, but when the time comes and the pile of mail just seems too overwhelming, then you might want to start putting them in a shoebox if you want to keep them. It is up to you what you do with the information.

You may also get magazines in the mail that talk about colleges and admissions processes. These are good because they give you an outside view of universities and procedures of those universities. It is sort of like an outlook for your future, which is good. Now I will tell you I do not think any of the information is going to be written by a college student, so they will have a different view on things. I have a more inside view because I am still in college. I went through what you are going through and what you will encounter, only about four years ago. Reading the information that they provide can be useful and even if it is not, it is good practice. It will help prepare you for some of the literature you have to read in college.

When you are trying to decide what university you want to go to, you should ask yourself some questions. Is this school the right school for me? Is it too far from home? Is it too close to home? Does this university offer my major? (Some schools have programs that require you to attend their university for X amount of years and then go to another school for the remaining number of years. My viewpoint on that issue is that the first time you come across something like this, think about attending the universities that have the full program for the certain major). Is this school too big for me? Is this school too small? Is my major one of their top programs? (You will find at every university, there are certain majors that they are sort of built around. The school is best known for this major. They have other majors, but none of them are looked upon as well as these one or two majors.)

You should check into what that school is best known for. I suggest you to go to the schools that are known for having a good program for what you want to major in, and that way you know you are getting a quality education. Does this university have a full-ride program? (Full rides are scholarships that pay for everything: tuition, room and board, fees…some of them even pay for books. This is an excellent topic to look into.) Has this university offered me any scholarships? What is the ratio of males to females? What is the ratio of students to teachers? What percent of teachers have a Ph.D.? (This is a good question to ask yourself, but just some words of wisdom: Just because a teacher has a Ph.D. does not automatically make him or her a good teacher. Some of my best teachers do not have PhD's.) What type of housing do they offer? Do all students live in dormitories or do all students live in apartments? All of these questions are good, but the main question that you should be concerned with is, "Is the program for my major very good at this university?" A school's program includes: the professor: student ratio, the graduation rate, the percentage of students that get jobs within four months after graduation, the type of companies that recruit from the school, the number of companies that recruit from the school, the opportunities for post-graduate education and the type of funding the program receives. If the school does not have a very good program for your major, then you may want to consider other universities that have a better program.

You will also have the opportunity to go to college fairs for these next couple of years. I highly recommend that you go to as many college fairs as you possibly can. This is your chance. You have the opportunity to speak to someone who works at that school, and has probably been there for a long time. What better way to learn about a university than to talk to someone who is always there? You can ask them any questions about that school. They can give you the up-close and personal view. Depending on how good they are, they can put the image of the university in your head as if you were already a student attending classes, and they can tell you all the different experiences you may come in contact with.

One thing that I try to do is to give you as many angles of situations as I can. I want you to know the good, the bad, and the ridiculous, and I cannot leave this one at just the good. The flip side of the coin is "deadbeat" representatives. They do not know a lick about the school; they really couldn't care less about being at the college fair. All they want to do is say hi, hand you a flyer, and hope that you walk past and not ask them any questions. Do not let them discourage you from talking to people. If that school only has one representative, and they are not helping you at all, go on to the next school that you are interested in. This is bad for the university, because employees like that are what will cause freshman entry rates to go down. You want to talk to someone who will take their time with you and explain all you want to know about the schools that you want to go to. Go up to them and ask them some questions. I don't care if you do not ask them anything else, but you must at least walk up to them and introduce yourself and say, "Would you tell me about the scholarship programs your university has? Is there a full-ride or presidential scholarship offered?" Once you find out about the money, and they say something that impresses you, I promise more questions will rapidly begin rolling off your tongue.

In Lansing, Michigan, where I am from, different organizations take students to college tours. Every year it was a different group of students, and sometimes even a different group of schools. They would go to anywhere between five and ten different universities doing campus tours and talking to different people on campus. Find out if there is such a thing in your town. If there is and they are going to visit one of the schools that you are interested in, you should go. I recommend that you go with just your parent(s), because when you go with them you will have the opportunity to talk to different representatives one-on-one and you can get more personal attention. But if you can't and it is your only chance to go to that certain university, then you should go with the tour because then you will get an actual view of the campus and the college life it holds. You may even get a chance to speak with some students who attend that university and they can give you a "real deal" about the school.

Pre-college programs are the best. Almost all of the universities that I have come in contact with offer some type of summer program for high school students. The programs are geared toward enlightening young minds toward the ways of college life, the type of activities that college students participate in, and how it feels to live in a college dorm. They are basically programs to give you the overall college experience, except for the classes. I know that you are thinking that the classes are the most important part of going to college. This is true, but the sooner you get all the bugs of "finally being in college" out of your system, the sooner you will solely focus on school. These pre-college programs do that. Participating in them helps you get the college bugs out of your system before you even go to college.

If you are thinking about getting into one of these programs, I recommend that you get in a program that is being offered at the university that is closest to your home. You can go to college anywhere in the world, but you don't really need to travel far for the pre-college programs. You are just trying to get the "basic" feel of college life and actually, you don't necessarily have to go to the school you are planning to attend after you graduate to do that.

If you are planning to go to an Ivy League school, you will probably get the opportunity to interview with someone associated with that university. You will either go to their house or they will come to yours, and you will actually sit down and talk to them about the university. It is almost like the college fairs if you think about it, but instead of them talking to a lot of different students, they are focusing particularly on you.

It is not tough or even a reason to get nervous. It is a very laid back environment where you all just talk. They will probably take notes and ask a lot of questions, but it is really no big deal. They have to report back to the university and tell them if you impressed them or not. That is a very nice chance to get personal with someone who is familiar with the school, and they should be able to answer a lot of your questions too.

Just recently, while writing this book, I was on the Internet surfing around. I wasn't looking for anything in particular, but ironically, I usually find the most useful information when I am just arbitrarily surfing for no reason. I came upon this Web site: *www.colleges. com.* At first I didn't really think much of it, I figured it was just another gimmick Web site that would not be too useful to me. One second I was ready to keep on searching and skip past this site, and then I thought about it. The information on this site may be somewhat useful to my readers. With that, I decided to indulge further into the site to see if it was worth my while, and even more importantly, worth yours.

The information that I found while I searched was priceless. I would not rate this a perfect Web site because it had its flaws, but I would highly recommend that you check this site out and look up some of the schools that you are interested in. I know that this book is mainly on scholarships, but a major part of your scholarship search goes hand-in-hand with the school you decide to go to. Some schools have enough money that you will not need outside scholarships, because they will pay for everything, but there are others that don't have that much money and therefore don't have the power to award as many students scholarships as they may want; or they can award a lot of students scholarships, but the amounts of the scholarships that they award are not that much. This Web site is not going to tell you if the school you have chosen is a rich school or a poor school, but it will tell you a lot of vital information that you can use to decide if that is the school you want to go to.

What I am saying is, among all the football games, basketball games, homecoming and prom, spend a little time on planning your future. Try to get as much information on colleges as you can, so that you will be happy with the university you choose to attend. I know when you are upperclassmen, besides the games and the parties, nothing else really matters, but you need to spend some time on the next phase of life. But, like I was saying earlier, treasure what you have because it's good. High school should just be fun. Nothing bad really happens, except for the occasional fight every once in a while and fights are so funny because the two people that fight really don't even have a clue why they are fighting. One thing is for sure, fighting is a very immature and that is one trait that you do not need to bring with you to college, leave that at high school. You have the teen clubs, the parties at school, and all that good stuff. These are your last years to experience that. Take heed because once you are done, that is it, no more high school. You will feel like your life has ended and then began again all in one summer.

VI. College Life: Advice 101

Amidst the warmth of the ending summer, subtle leaves slowly falling to the foundational ground. A world that seems so different, but looks so much the same. Look at the sky, it's as blue as the deepest sea. The clouds are white, fluffy, and in shapes that you swear you have seen somewhere before. Observe the wind, it is as calm as a mother aiding her children.

Voices coming from afar, footsteps in this newfound area of life, enjoying the breeze of this long-anticipated day, you take a moment to just stand silently observing your surroundings. As you look around, you begin noticing all of these buildings everywhere and you have no clue in the world what anything is. People wandering around like lost souls with no idea where they are going. You hear car stereos booming as they turn the corner; grocery bag after grocery bag, suitcase after suitcase, it's the end of everyone's vacation except yours. For you this is something different. For you this is something very new. This is the beginning of college life. You are now a college freshman and you have finally stepped foot on the campus where you will spend the next four to five years earning your education and planning your future. You do not have to worry about getting any loans because of all the scholarships you have earned. You are finally free from your parents. It starts feeling like party time, but there is one problem.

You do not know anything about college. You have no idea where your classes are; you do not know your way around campus. What are you going to do? You don't know anybody. All of your friends are at different schools. You do not have your identification yet. Where are you going to eat, how are you going to find your classes? You are so far away from home. Your parents just dropped you off and left you. You are all alone and do not have a clue. WHAT ARE YOU GOING TO DO!

Don't worry--these questions, thoughts and more go through the mind of each and every student who has ever stepped foot on campus as a college freshman. You are not alone. I bet if you walk up to someone and started talking, you would find that they too are lost, they don't know anybody, and they are new. There are a lot of freshmen and usually they all have the same, "I don't know what the heck is going on" look on their face. This is not high school anymore. You don't have the luxury of having all of your classes in the same building. You don't have the opportunity to go home and eat food that your mother has in the fridge. You are officially on your own; headed on the path to adulthood. Breathe in that fresh air. Take a deep breath; let it out. How does it feel?

Remember when you were little, going around telling everybody, "I'm grown, I can handle myself." Do you still feel that way? Are you grown? Yes. Can you handle yourself? Yes, but are you a little nervous? I know "little" doesn't come close to how you are feeling right now. Your parents just left you at school...ALL ALONE. That's terrible! You can't go bug them when you want to, you can't go ask them for money and expect it that instant like you used to, but all of that is OK; this is a part of growing up. Don't worry about it; once classes start rolling you will be OK. You are finally in college. Can you believe it? All those years of elementary school, middle school, and high school were all to prepare you for this: college. You are going to experience some things this semester that will blow your mind, and people, you will meet people who will make you say to yourself, "I thought I had it bad, my life was nothing compared to theirs". You will also meet some people who are just wild; it seems like all they do is party. Don't fall in that trap.

The biggest advice that I can ever give to a college student is this: Surround yourself with people who are just like you or people who are on the road to success. If you like to study at two in the morning, then you need to hang with people who like to stay up late and study, but if you are like me and you do your best work between the hours of seven and nine in the morning, then you don't want to study with those students, because they will get you off track. The biggest misconception of all high school students is they think they do not have good study habits. You have heard it on television, in class, and from different speakers. Your mind has been bogged down so much with the words, *develop good study habits*, that you don't think you have any. The only bad study habits are NO study habits. There is no one perfect way to study.

The way I study is good for me; it works for me, and I like to study that way. But my roommate junior year could not study like that. He and I are in the same major, chemical engineering, the same classes, and we never studied together. When he was studying, I would be trying to get some sleep or on my way out somewhere, and every time I was studying, he would not be around.

Some people study well with note cards, others study better by reading the textbook over and over again. What suits you best is the way you should study. I am not saying don't try to improve your study habits, because you should. Studying is one process that can always be improved. It is good to try different methods, just don't try them at the wrong times. Let me explain. If your friends come to you one day and tell you about this new way of studying that has been helping them a lot, try it, see if it works for you, but only try it on the nights that you don't have anything big to do in that class the next day. Instead of telling you when to try it, I will tell you when not to try to implement new habits. Don't wait until the week before finals to try new habits. These are your finals, you need to study the way that helped you do your best in the past; it's too late to start something new. Actually, you shouldn't try anything new the day before any test. If you want to try it, try it a week or two before the test. Give yourself a comfort zone, just in case it does not work the way you thought it might; then, as the test date gets closer and closer, you can decide if you want to try a new way, or if you feel your old way of studying would work out best.

I am not telling you any certain way that you should study, because I don't want to lead you down the wrong path, but I will give you some ideas of different study habits that may work. The way you know that your method of studying is good is if you are getting A's on everything. Oh yeah, cheating is not an option. You can cheat your way all through college, but when you get out, you are not going to know anything, and it will show when you get to the interviews for your jobs. Even if you do get the job because of your interview skills, if you get hired and you cannot perform the way that they expect you ought to be able to, you will lose that job. Keep this in mind next time you think about cheating. Here are some study habits that may work for you.

One way of studying is to study each and every subject for about 30 minutes a day. You have to study even when you do not think you have anything to study. You always have the option to briefly go through some future chapters that you are going to cover in class, or you can always review past chapters that you have talked about in class. Another idea is study groups. Meet in groups of people and have them ask you questions about different topics in class. You get a chance to interact with others, and you will learn some things from them that you may not have picked up in class. Studying alone is sometimes good too, because when people study in groups, it does not always work well. Everybody gets together with studying in mind, then all kinds of other conversations strike up and the study group turns into party central.

Studying alone gives you the opportunity to be without outside interruptions. It gives your mind the ease of depending only on your work and you can think without distractions from outside sources. Individual studying has its downfalls too, because if you get stuck somewhere, you don't have anyone to ask and a lot of times, you may find yourself frustrated to the point where you just do not want to study anymore. So you have to watch out for that too.

Places to study are the key to the quality of your studying. You will have access to the library and other buildings on campus to go to and study. You will also have your room. These are all excellent places because the library gives you access to all the other students who are there, even when you are studying by yourself. Your room gives you the comfort of being in your own zone, and other buildings get you away from everything. At the library, you run the risk of people constantly coming up to you, trying to start a conversation with you, and you have the constant desire of going to the nearest computer to check your e-mail or other Web sites.

In your room, you have the television right there, and you will constantly try to tell yourself that age-old lie, "I can study just as good with the TV on as I can with it off." And you have your telephone, which is obviously going to constantly ring. You will find that more people want to hang out when you are trying to actually study than any other time that you're in school.

The other buildings are good because you don't have a phone and you don't have a TV, you don't have computers, and you don't have anyone coming up to you bugging you while you're trying to study. But what you will have, each time you decide to take a 30-

second break, is a brisk feeling of boredom rushing at you, and the ideas of the hundred million other things you could be doing if you were not studying. That can render fierce agony on your study time. For all of these places and ideas for studying, there are negatives, but also positives. Not everyone will experience the negatives. You may have a way of studying which is only positive. When you find that way, when your mind is composed and you study well in that environment, continue studying that way. That is what you are searching for.

Now that we have talked about studying, let's get back to people. There are all kinds of people in college. I am talking about people who can party harder, study more, sleep less and still get good grades, but there are also those who never party, always study, and still fail. This is my second best advice that I can give to a college student. Make your life 60/40. Sixty percent of your college life should be spent solely on education. This does not include going to class. Going to class is a must, so do not ever skip a class, and even worse, do not ever fall asleep in class. But for the time that you are not in class, you need to lead a 60/40 life. What is the 40 percent? It's quite simple actually. The 40 percent is actually social time. A lot of parents may not agree with me, but trust me you need 40. I live by the model "work before play" and you should too, but you need to at least spend 40 percent of your time playing.

Now this does not mean split each and every day of your college life into 60 percent and 40 percent and make it a point that every day at a certain time, you stop all studying and start playing. This also doesn't mean spend 4.2 days a week studying and 2.8 days just partying. We need to get that straight too, but the reason I am saying this is because I think in extremes. An extreme case of one hundred percent studying will make a person go crazy. They will either end up in the nuthouse or committing suicide, and on the other hand, one hundred percent partying will mess up a person's head. They will either end up in jail or dropped out of school.

I do not want you to end up like either of these extreme cases. Sixty-forty is more realistic. You should always spend a little more time studying and doing educational activities while you are in college because that is the whole purpose of going. The 40 percent should be the time that you spend playing sports, going to parties, and watching television. At first, 40 percent seems like a lot, but it really isn't. This is just the time that you can relax and not think about what you have to turn in the next day, what is going to be on the test, and how you are going to finish your paper. All that needs to be done first, then the 40 percent "play time" can take effect and just chill. Everybody loves to play cards and dominoes; it's like a favorite past time for college students. Make sure you get involved in social activities because they help you mellow out your brain, and give it a little time to rest so that when you need it later, you won't be too stressed to study.

Do not go over the limit of 40 percent, because you will start treading dangerous waters. When you get to the point that you feel like you are partying just as much as you are studying, then you need to slow it down. It is a whole lot easier to stop studying and just party all the time, but usually after a while, that starts to get old and you will be bored of partying. The irony of that is, by the time you start getting bored of partying, it will be too late to bring your grades up, and you will notice everyone else around you was keeping up with their school work and you will be stuck and left out. Make sure you get enough extracurricular activities to ease your mind from the tension of school every once in a while.

One serious issue about college is that everyone you see your freshman year will not graduate. You will notice that every year, actually every semester, more and more students will seem to have disappeared from campus. There are a very small percentage of students who actually transfer and keep their stride of education going, but a lot of the people who are gone don't return to school at all. Do not let this affect you. There were three guys I used to hang out with all the time when I was a freshman. I used to go to their dorm room and we used to always kick it. Didn't matter if it was on the Playstation, walking around campus, or talking to girls at parties, I was always with at least one of them. In my senior year, my fourth year, none of those three remained at my school. Can you imagine that? Out of all the people I chose as my friends, none of those three remained at my school. I know they all transferred out at different times, but I have no idea if any of them are still in school.

There are going to be students who are 27 years old who are still trying to get their bachelor's degree. I can understand those who decided to go back to school at 27, but they were people who were 27 years old and had been in college every semester since they graduated high school, that is crazy. By the time you are 27 you should either be working somewhere or in your Ph.D. program. It should not take you any more, and I mean at the very most, five years to graduate, and that's if you fail a class or two. All students in college should graduate in four years. There is a way to do it in every major and I know you can do it. You may have to take a lot of classes each semester, but you can do it. I believe you can.

If you have made it this far in this book, that means you are a goal seeker and you have the motivation to research information and find what you need to succeed. You have the values and you have dedication. With those two qualities, you can make anything happen. So if that means that you are the youngest person in your graduating class, then so be it. Let's talk about students.

This is the place that all those peer pressure commercials were warning you about. I used to hear about peer pressure in middle school and in high school. They used to talk to us about all the ways our "so-called" friends would try to talk us into smoking weed, drinking, and other stuff like that, but I had never actually experienced it. As a matter of fact, it got to the point where I did not even believe that peer pressure actually existed. My eyes were opened and mind made clear when I finally got into college. It was like a wake-up call or culture shock. I mean it wasn't like I was eased into it. No, the whole peer pressure house came crashing down and I was standing directly underneath it. I was OK because my mother instilled such qualities and values that were needed to see past all of the dangerous ways of "having fun," but I would be lying if I said I wasn't challenged to go against my upbringing.

By the time I was going to college, I had been so good, everybody forgot to tell me that I might come in contact with this stuff in college. Maybe it was just that I was so naïve or that I just didn't want to believe it, but there wasn't anything stopping the pressure blows from every angle coming at me. I felt like a ninja having to block all that stuff. Here I was thinking peer pressure stopped at high school. You need this warning. It will save you from the sudden enlightenment that you will receive without it.

Peer pressure is crazy in college. It's not going to be somebody you don't know at a party or just some crazy kid. No, the people who will be pressuring you are going to be those people who helped you find your way around campus, the students who were so nice and sweet that you thought they were going to be cool to kick it with. You thought they were angels. It will be those you call your friends, the ones whom you would tell anything to because they have gained so much trust. Watch out for them.

I'm not saying go to school and don't make any friends. That would be crazy. You should get cool with as many people as you can because you never know when you will see them again. One of them might be the person to help you get that job or that bonus. All I am saying is if you are at a party or something and someone tries to talk you into doing something that you don't want to do, just say no. I know you are thinking, "Come on man, I've heard this a thousand times. If they try to talk me into doing something that I don't want to do, say no, duh!" You may be thinking that, but what you don't realize is that by the time you get to college your curiosity may become a millions times higher than it is right now, and that is what makes you vulnerable. Your mind will start telling you things like, "It's not that bad. Come on, you're an adult now. Just try it once, and if I don't like it, don't do it again." Thoughts like that will go through your brain to the point where you can get confused.

I know some of you are thinking, "Well, what if I do just want to try it once?" Let me tell you now, once you start something it will be hard to stop. Let me tell you why. Let's say for instance, you take your first drink of alcohol, just for curiosity's sake. If you like it, what are you going to do? You are going to keep drinking; you have just picked up a bad habit. Now let's flip it, if you drink that same drink, but you hate it. You are still going to drink a little more and a little more because your curiosity will hit you and say something like, "Maybe if I drink some more, I will start tasting what they taste. It probably just tastes nasty because it's my first time. Well let me just take one more drink and if I don't like it then I will stop." As you see, it's a big circle pattern. My advice to you is, whatever you don't like to do now, don't start doing in college.

That is enough about people, now let's talk about classes. My freshman year was the worst because I didn't know anything about credit hours, prerequisites, or anything like that, and I was completely lost. After you choose your major, you will find out how many credit hours you need to graduate with that degree. Credit hours are what you get from each class that you take. The number of credit hours per class designates how many hours you have to take that class per week.

Now let us say that you have a three credit hour class. What that means is that you have that class for three hours a week. Each major has a set amount of credit hours needed to graduate. That is decided by how many credit hours each class you have to take to graduate has. Prerequisites are classes that you have to take before you can take a certain class. For example, let's say you want to take organic chemistry. You will find that before you can take organic you have to not only take general chemistry I and II, but you also have to pass both classes. Therefore general chemistry I and II are prerequisites for organic chemistry.

What I most treasure about my freshman year was an assignment from my creative engineering course. We had to sketch out our college plan. In this plan, we had to indicate what courses we were going to take each semester and how much it would cost: books, pens, pencils, classes, transportation, clothing, everything. I treasure that very much because it forced me to learn the system and figure out a way for me to graduate within four years. Because I waited until that course to do that I was already locked into the system, forcing me to take some summer courses.

The reason I am telling you this is because I want you to get a head start. The best way to succeed in something is to plan. Once you have decided what your major is going to be, get a catalog from the school. Do this before school starts, like during the summer before your first semester. A section that covers your major will be in that catalog. You will be able to see all the classes that you are going to have to take to graduate, and you will find what courses have prerequisites and what classes are prerequisites. Some classes are even co-requisites which means they must be taken together. When you get this, chart out a plan for yourself.

I will give you an example by using my program. To graduate from Prairie View A&M University with a B.S. in chemical engineering, in accordance with the fall nineteen ninety-eight catalog (at some universities, new catalogs are composed every year, you have to abide by the catalog that most current your first year of school), a student must earn 141 credits. The only way I could graduate in four years was to take 17 to 19 credit hours each semester. That averages out to about five to eight classes. To some people, this is a lot. To be recognized as a full-time student, you have to take at least 12 credit hours. The average student takes about 15, so that will give you a range of how classes are.

You need to decide what amount of classes is right for you. Are 18 or 19 credits too much for you? Will 12 be enough? It is hard to decide this, since you have not been in college yet, so I say just look at the number of credits you need to graduate, divide that by eight, (because four years is eight semesters). This is the average amount of credits you must take each semester to graduate in four years.

Keep in mind, when you are making your plan that some classes are going to require prerequisites. Make sure those prerequisites are in the accurate place in your graduation plan to ensure that you will not be held back a semester. It may seem tough at first, but I promise you it will be worth it and it will help your semesters go smoothly. While students are still trying to figure out what to take, you will be enrolling and you will be soon graduating in the amount of time that you planned.

One thing about college is that a class is only as good as its professor. I was lucky when I got to school, because when I went to go fill out my schedule, this young lady who worked in my department was a junior and she had already taken the classes I was about to take. She went through the schedule book with me and told me which professors were good and which professors I should definitely not take. I tell you, if it was not for her, I have no idea where I would be right now. Probably stuck in my sophomore year.

When you get to school, you are already going to have your plan for the next four years, and if you don't, make sure that is the first thing you do. Once you are ready to choose the professor for your classes, find someone who is an upperclassman, a junior or a senior, you can actually even talk to sophomores. Find someone who has already taken the classes that you are going to take, and ask them about some of the professors in the schedule book. If they give you good details about certain professors, tell you which ones to take and which ones definitely not to take, then take their advice; they are really trying to help. You may run into somebody and they will be so "busy" that they just blow you off and not tell you anything. If this happens, don't worry about it, just find somebody else. Never let one person's pain become your stress.

The best place to start is in your department. The department is the office area of your major. That Is where your department head is, and there are usually students who work there who are in your major. If there isn't anyone there, or you come across the situation that another freshman is working there, you can just walk around the building that your department is in and ask somebody who is just in the hallway.

There are a lot of types of professors out there. Some teach straight from the book, word for word, and some don't bring a book to class the whole year. You will even have some professors who will say that you do not need to buy the book for that class, and still some who will make you buy the book and then teach out of a totally different book. So don't go out and rush to buy books when you get to school. They are very expensive, and you will feel really dumb if you buy a book and then you find out that you are not going to need it. You may find out early enough that you can take it back and get a full refund on it, but why take that chance? It's not going to be a rush. There are some bad professors out there who seem like they don't even know their subject, but you won't come across them too often. What you will come across is even worse. These are professors who know the material. I mean you can flip through the book and ask them a question from any random page and they can give you a detailed answer for that question, but for the life of them, they cannot stand in front of a class and teach students in a way they can understand. These are teachers who know the book, back and forth, but cannot teach at all. They are just terrible at it. I am not saying that they are nervous in front of a group of people. What they have is worse; it is like they are so smart that they don't know how to share their intelligence. Hopefully you can get through college without having to take one of these types of professors, but if you do get one, you will remember what I said and then understand what I meant.

The first couple of days in school, and this goes for every school, the professors, nine times out of ten, are not going to go into any detail about the subject. Usually they spend that first one or two days of class explaining the syllabus (a packet that explains what the course covers), what book you will use (if any), when tests will be, grading procedures, and just an overall background of the class. The reason they don't usually teach is because for the first couple of days, students are still trying to find out where their classes are, and a lot of students are adding and dropping classes. Professors only like to teach to the students who are going to remain in the course the entire semester; they usually don't have this group the first one or two days of class.

It's good to go because you need to get an early feel of what the class is going to be like. Remember, you are going to be there for the next 18 weeks or so. Find somebody in class who you can be cool with because you may need to study with someone one day. It is also good because if you can't make it to class one day because you are sick or going out of town, you are going to need someone to tell you what was covered in class. You can have someone you can call a friend in every class because they are the ones who will go into detail about what was covered, what the assignments are (if there is an assignment), when the next test is going to be, and what will be on it.

Making friends is very important in college. I don't know anyone who made it through college without having any friends. I actually don't know anyone who would want to, but like I said earlier, your friends are usually the ones who get you into trouble. Just make sure that they know your boundaries, and even better, make sure that they respect your boundaries. You should not have any problems if you do that because even though friends get you in trouble sometimes, they are always there to watch out for you and make sure nothing really bad happens to you.

People always say that college is so much harder than high school. I would not go as far to say that college is so much tougher than high school, as it is just different. The differences between high school and college are what really cause the illusion that it is harder. I guarantee that if there was such a thing as thirteenth grade in high school and it had all the same classes that you would take your freshman year of college, you would pass those classes with ease because you won't be thinking about all the other things that differ in college and high school. Well, what is so different?

Besides the fact that you are away from home, you do not have all of your classes in the same building, and you probably don't know anybody, probably not much, but really those big differences are not what counts. It is the little things that matter. You don't have your mother to wake you up in the morning to tell you it is time to go to school. You do not have your mother to cook you breakfast anymore. You have to fend for yourself. You don't have the same classes every day. Either you will have a class on Monday, Wednesday, and Friday or you will have that class on Tuesday and Thursday.

When you are in college, you are not going to have a chore list. So whatever you do not clean just does not get cleaned, and if you have a dirty roommate, you may find that the bathtub does not get cleaned when they get out of it. You are going to have some professors who know you by name, and you will have other professors who make it a point not to know you by your name. Half of them will not care if you come to class anyway; they already have your money. While you are in college, there are going to be a lot of times when you can't find anything to do, or there will be things to do, but none of them interest you and you will basically force yourself into boredom. There will also be times at school when there is so much to do, so many activities that you want to participate in but you can't because they are all happening at the same time. Prepare yourself for both, because they will occur, along with the time when there are things to do but you have to study. That is the worst.

College food is another story. At least when you were in high school, you only had to dread what the cafeteria was serving for lunch. In college, unless you have your own apartment and you enjoy cooking, you are going to eat cafeteria food every time you are hungry. You might as well start liking it, because you are going to be eating this stuff for at least four years. Let's say, for example, you are one of those lucky students who live off campus. You are going to have to cook for yourself every day, every meal. I would rather have the choice of going to the cafeteria to get food, than having to cook for myself all the time; especially when I was a freshman.

College is your transition point. You are right in between a time of no responsibility and a life full of responsibilities. While you are in college, not only are you getting more education, but you are also growing up. You are becoming an adult and you need to develop your maturity as well. It says a lot that you are reading this book right now; it shows you are maturing. That journey of maturity will continue on when you are in school. Even though you are going to college, don't think that you are going to a place of harder education. Think of it as a more challenging education. You can handle it and it is not that difficult, but you must put your energy and your desires into wanting that education and striving for that education, because if you don't, it will be your downfall.

I cannot talk about college without talking about your living space. The space in a college dorm is about one upgrade from a jail cell. It is the worst. The luxury days of sleeping in a queen size or king size bed are long gone. Even if you only had a full size bed, you were still better off. All college dorms have twin size beds. If you are trying to figure out what size sheets to get, just get twin, because that is what you are going to be sleeping on for a while. You may get the luxury of getting an extended twin size bed, but it is still going to be a twin, just a little longer.

The room is small and you have to share it with somebody else. At some schools you have to share that same room with two other people. I can almost guarantee that your college dorm is going to be less spacious than your bedroom at home, but there is a reason for that. The college dorm room is not there for you to sit around and be bored all day. They make them small because they want to encourage students to get out of the room and go meet some people. Many dormitories have lounge areas on the first floor. There is usually a lot of space there and they have a television. Don't make the mistake of being stuck in your dorm room all day. The only time I'm usually in mine is when I am sleeping and sometimes when I am studying. That is what they are for.

When you are in college, you are going to notice that there are groups of people who always hang around each other. Some of them even have shirts and hats with Greek letters. The groups of women are called sororities and the groups of men are called fraternities. They all have their own foundations, aims, and mottos. The membership has its benefits and I say that if it is something that you want to do, then you should pursue it. But, just as you do with anything else that you do not know much about, you need to take some time out and research that organization before you decide to join. They are lifelong organizations and you want to know exactly what you are getting into before you join. There are all kinds of books in the library that can help you do some research about that organization and there are a number of Web sites that you can go to. If you are interested in looking at some Web sites, go to *www.greekpages.com,* a good resource for fraternity and sorority information. It splits the organizations up by university or by name of the organization, and you can go to different Web sites to learn what they are about. There are other organizations that may interest you that are co-ed. Most co-ed organizations are honor societies or other organizations within a certain major. You can talk to your department head about those. You can even talk to other students who may know something about them.

I am not trying to scare you or make you think that college life is just too crazy to handle, because it is not. I have experienced some of my best times In life while I have been in college. Sometimes I think of college like FantasyIsland. You really do not have any responsibilities. All you have to do is pay for school and go to class and that is it. There are no other bills you have to worry about and no kids you have to watch. This is the first time since I have been in school that I can be done with all my classes by noon. Can you believe that? I know you can't, I couldn't either. If you want, you can go to your room in the middle of the day and rest for a while or you can go somewhere else on campus and kick it. I know every school has a popular spot, and I'm sure you will find out where it is very soon. It is OK to go out sometimes and chill. As long as you don't make chilling and kicking it your favorite thing to do you will be all right.

There is no party like a college party. I can promise you that. When you are in college, the parties are like mini-Cancuns. If you drink, usually you have access to all the free drinks that you can handle, and if you don't drink, you can still dance all night and listen to the music they are playing. You have to experience at least one party per semester just so you can get the whole feel of college life. Sometimes you will meet people at parties that you end up being very good friends with. I am a very versatile person, and one of my favorite mottos is, "I will try anything once, as long as it is not crazy and it won't put my life in danger." A party will not put your life in danger. Just make sure that you don't take any drugs, and at parties do not drink if they won't let you make your own drink. Do not ever drink something that someone else has made for you. You have no idea what they put in your drink, so if they refuse to let you make your own, then don't drink at all.

If you are at a party and you get yourself a drink, if you ever put your drink down, it does not matter if you put it down to dance or to go to the bathroom, do not pick that drink back up and drink from it again. You always have to watch out for yourself. When people have liquor in their system, they do some wild things. Somebody could put anything in your drink when you sit it down. They might not put drugs in your drink, but they may spit in it or put bugs in it. There are all kinds of things that they can do. Just live by this: if you are going to drink at a party, one, make your own drink and two, don't put it down unless you do not plan on drinking from that cup anymore.

The reason people think that college is so tough is because there is so much to do at school that can take away from your goal of studying. Organizations, trips, friends, and parties can all take away from study time, and the fact that you are still learning information that you have never seen before will also cause this misconception. Find what study habits work best for you. If you get to college and realize that the way you were studying in high school is still a very good way to study, then continue that, but if you are realizing that the way you studied in high school is not going to do it, then you need to find something that will work for you. Make sure that you get a head start in planning your college education. The earlier you start planning your graduation plan, the more prepared you will be each semester.

Don't forget that your whole purpose in going to college is to get your degree and then get out. Do not make being a college student your occupation. Trust me, it does not pay well. There is no reason that, while going to college every semester directly after graduating from high school, you should be getting close to 30 and not have your first degree.

Peer pressure is a big deal at college. I know you may feel that you can deal with anything right now because you are a high school upperclassman, but I am here to tell you that you will be tempted. Keep the same focus and don't let temptation attack your curiosity, and if it does get to your curiosity, don't let your curiosity get to you. Remember; keep your college career at a 60/40 pattern. Sixty percent of your college life should be focused on studying, knowing your information, preparing for tests, writing papers, etc., and forty percent of your time should be spent hanging out, going out, playing sports, working out, and even going to a party every once in a while. You have to have that balance because I do not want you to go crazy, and I don't want you to stress yourself out. If you keep that balance, you won't ever have to worry about it.

College life is a lot different from high school life. There are a few major differences, but you are going to find out that most of the differences that really count are small differences, and you can handle it. Make sure that you check out the different organizations on campus. If you find an organization that interests you, research it and see if you really want to become a member. Look at some of the activities they do, and meet some of the people. You don't want to be in an organization where you don't like anybody or one that does activities that you absolutely hate. If you find out that you don't even want to be a part of any organization, that is cool too.

The dorm rooms may be small, but that's OK; don't spend all your time in your room. Enjoy the parties, but make sure that you enjoy them in a safe way. Do what is best for you because the only person you are really going to affect right now is you.

VII. Money after Freshman Year

So how was it? Your freshman year is finally over. Did you make it? Are you still the same person you were before you went to college? Did you keep your grades up? Are all those scholarships that you got your freshman year going to carry over to your sophomore year? If they are not, then we have some work to do. The hardest time to get scholarships for college is when you are a high school senior about to become a freshman. It is so easy to get more money. All you have to do is keep your grade point average up. As long as you have at least a three-point, you are OK. A three-point is a B average from the standpoint of letter grades, but in college that means that you are working hard and you are trying to do well. If you have a three point five or higher, you can basically write your own ticket because the majority of students don't have that.

Where do you get scholarships after your freshman year? There are two main places you should start looking for scholarships after your freshman year: your department and the scholarship office. If your school does not have a scholarship office, then you should go to the financial aid department. Just like the other scholarships, you want to get them early. Even though you do not need the money until the fall semester after your freshman year, you should go to the office in January, a week or two after you get back from Christmas break. In life, it is always better to get a head start on your goals, or any projects that you do. It isn't any different with scholarships. When you go to those offices, ask somebody what types of scholarships they are offering for the next semester and when the deadlines are. This way you will know for sure when you need to start trying to apply for this money and you can make sure you get it.

You should also continue checking *www. fastweb.com.* Fastweb is a good Web site because it stays up to date with your classification (the year of college you are in), and it will find scholarships for you for the following year. You need to check it at least once a month. Deadlines for scholarships, outside of school, are most often during the end of January, all of February, and the beginning of March. You want to always know when your application is due so you can prepare you essays and have everything ready for the next year.

By the time this book comes out, I'm sure there will be more and better Websites than *www.fastweb.*

com, but since it has worked so well for me, I am recommending it. If you find something that is better than Fastweb, don't worry about using Fastweb. Make sure the site that you use is free. There is absolutely no reason whatsoever that you should pay for scholarship information. A lot of people say that it takes money to make money. That may be true in some cases, but that is not the case with scholarships. You earn scholarship money with hard work and real effort. You should not have to pay for anything. If you ever come across something that is trying to charge you, do not pay for it. Why should you? The information is for anyone who researches it. You are a college student now. You need to fine tune your research skills anyway, so why pay for somebody to do the work for you. If you do stoop down to that level of paying to become a member of some Web site just to get scholarships, two things will happen: one, you will spend money that you don't need to spend and two, it will erase all the value that you have on hard work, and you do not want that. Hard work is a value that everybody needs and you are no exception.

Don't forget about all those books that you had researched while you were in high school. Remember all the times that you found a scholarship, but you couldn't apply for it because it asked for returning college students or students entering their sophomore year. Well now you can apply for all of those scholarships. As you find them, instead of passing them by, take them down as notes and keep them in a folder so that you can go back to them in future years to apply.

The best way to get scholarship money from college departments is to impress the personnel in such a way that they will tell you about scholarships without you even asking. There is a way to do that and it is very simple. Before I get into that, let me tell you this: Do not, in any circumstances, act in a way that is not you. To get people who are in charge of scholarships to notice you is basically to be yourself. Take all of your courses seriously and try to get A's in all of them. It is OK if you don't get A's, but you have to at least try. Constantly ask them about scholarships and what they are offering in the future. What you are doing is setting the foundation for them to know that you are a good student and that you are interested in getting scholarships.

Sometimes you should go to their offices and just talk to them. You can talk to these individuals about whatever. Try to have some conversations with them where you do not say anything about scholarships. This goes back to just being friendly, and it is also the way they start to get familiar with your personality and get to know you personally. You want it to reach the point that when you walk in the office, they won't be thinking, "There's that student who always bugs me about scholarships." When I walk in, they say, "Hi Charles, how are you doing?" and that's how it should be with you. You want them to know your first name. When they start to know you personally, they will start noticing how you are a good student and they will see all the hard work you put into school. They will realize that you are very persistent and you are goal-oriented.

When they realize that you set goals and achieve them, they also realize how good a student you are. You will begin to become friends with them and you won't have to worry about asking them about scholarships, because they will automatically start

126

telling you. This is what you want. Once you get to that point, you will be in good hands and you will start getting a lot of scholarships for the upcoming years that you are in school. To have those individuals calling your house to inform you of new scholarships is a little much, but it can happen. If it doesn't, it is OK. As long as when you go to their office, they give you information on scholarships without having to ask for it, you have got it made.

Timing is the key in this situation. That is why I was saying that you should meet and get to know as many people as you can because they will help you succeed. If you ever hear someone saying they got their success by themselves with no one to there to help, they are lying. You cannot do it by yourself. It's good that you are taking all the right steps, but there are others involved. Somebody had to create the www.fastweb.com's and the studentadvantages. Somebody has to work in the scholarship office and college departments.

What you will find while you are in college is that a lot of students get work-study—a job on campus--to help pay for their education. The money made from this position goes toward paying for tuition, room and board, and whatever other costs students may have. I am telling you this because a lot of times, the students who work in those offices are in positions that can benefit you. They will be either the secretary or maybe just someone who files the scholarships in the scholarship office. Who is the first person to see information? The person in the office who separates them and puts them in files; these students are the first people to see what scholarships are going to be offered in the future. If you are cool with them, they also will tell you about this stuff.This is different from the secretaries or middleman I referred to earlier because when you contact a corporation, the person that answers the phone may not even be in the same business group or office building as the person directly in charge of the scholarship. At the university you are in the exact place where the scholarships are offered, you are talking exactly to the person who files them, and that is why I urge you to talk to the secretary here. Only at the university's "Scholarship office".

As I review the past writings, I notice that it seems like I am suggesting that you meet only people who can help you. It seems like I am saying don't be friends with a person unless you can get something from them or they can help you in some way. I do not mean that at all. You should not try to get to know somebody just because they can help you, but you shouldn't avoid meeting people who are in those positions either. All I am saying is when you get to school, make a lot of friends and be nice to everybody, because you never know who they are or who they are going to be. The person you sit next to in your mathematics course may end up being the CEO of the next major stock trading company or they could be the next homeless person living in gutters, but nonetheless be nice to that person.

College friends are friends for life. You will start to form a bond and that bond will never be broken. It is good to have friends in high places, because these friends will help you. Even more important, if you are in a high place and you have a friend who is trying to succeed, help them. Use all that is in your power to bring your friends up. Take the information that you have about scholarships and pass it on. Tell them about places that they too can go and find scholarships and all other types of information that will help them get their college education paid for. This is a two-sided coin and you have to let it flip on both sides: help and be helped. It is bad to be selfish and keep information that you have gained to yourself. You will find that helping others will open more doors for you in the future. You will begin to see all kinds of other opportunities arising for you. More scholarships will come to you just from helping people find the scholarships you have found, but only help because you want to. If you only help someone just because you want what you will get in return, you may not get anything.

You are going to run into people who are unfriendly. I mean these people just act like they cannot be nice to save their soul. There is a reason for this, and it usually does not have anything to do with you. You cannot let someone being mean to you cause you to be mean to someone else. You should not even be rude or mean to that person. It is easier to bring thunderstorms to a sunny day than it is to warm up a cold heart, but your persistence in trying to find something good about them will make you a better person, and you will feel good about yourself. Don't just do everything for yourself; sometimes you have to step back and help others. Scholarships will come to you and you will find that good things, in general, will happen to you because of it.

There really isn't much else after your first year of school. Instead of having to search through books, (which you can if you want to), you now can go pick up scholarships from the scholarship office and your department. If you find that neither place is helping you at all, you keep talking to them and they just don't seem to have the information or scholarships, and they are not willing to help you, then you need to go back to the drawing board. There's nothing better than some good old-fashioned hard work. Go back to the books and the Web sites and the businesses. The amount of scholarships that you receive depends entirely on you. Even if you get ten applications between the scholarship office and your department, and you feel you need fifteen, then reread Chapter Two. Most scholarships that you can get when you are a high school senior are still available to you when you are a returning college student. Another secret of success is to get in touch with all of the contact people of the scholarships that you have received for your first year and find out if they have a renewal process. Many of them will tell you just to reapply like you did the first time, but there are still a lot of scholarship programs out there that give recipients a shortcut to receiving the scholarship again. Call them and say, "Hi my name is _____, and I received the scholarship this year. Would you please tell me the process for renewing it next year?"

IT WORKS…

VIII. Be a S.C.H.O.L.A.R.

       I have tried to take all that I have just explained to you about financial aid, ways of getting it, where to look and how to go about applying, and put everything into one word. It took a while because I wanted something special, something that meant a lot to me and was a perfect fit for our topic of discussion. Then out of nowhere, in between my contemplation, it came to me: Scholar. The word in itself expresses the essence of being a productive person, someone who takes pride in their work, a person who will rise above the average to make sure that their work has successful progress. A scholar sees to it that their goals are reached. So I say to you:

BE A SCHOLAR.

S=SEARCH/SEEK

In your planning periods of your future, take the time out to search for scholarships, grants, and fellowships (for graduate students). Utilize all the possible venues of information. In this age of computer technology, the Internet is the first place you should begin your search. Start out by going to search engines like *www.hotbot.com, www.yahoo. com* and *www.mamma.com.* Once you get in these sites, type in "scholarships" and this will take you to all the different scholarships that are being offered. There will also be other Web sites that don't correlate to your search, but continue going through the sites to find which best fits you.

In many cases, the search sites will find different scholarships that universities have for their students. Find out if the university that you plan to go to has their scholarships on the Web. Also type in "scholarship searchers," this will lead you to Web sites such as *www. fastweb.com* and *www.studentadvantage.com.* These sites are excellent resources. They have you fill out information that may take you 20 minutes; once you've filled out all the requested information, the program searches its database for scholarships that fit you. In some cases, the Web site will allow you to actually apply online. Take advantage of such resources.

Along with the Internet, you need to access personal resources. Teachers, counselors, program coordinators, and even principals will all have good information on specific scholarships, and if they don't, they will be able to point you in the direction of someone who does. University representatives are also an excellent source. Seek out the person in charge of scholarships (many universities have an actual scholarship office, this is the first place I would look) and find out what types of scholarships they are offering for your entering semester. Ask if the university has a general scholarship application for entering freshmen. This application is usually what gets a student a full ride at a college or university. This gives the scholarship administrators, who in many cases are separate from the admissions officials (those who grant entry into the school) a chance to review your information and credentials personally, and then they can make a decision on how much money they plan to give you. People are the most vital resources because you can have a conversation with them, unlike the two other ways to search. REMEMBER it is these kinds of people who write the books, design the Web pages, write your letters of recommendation and most *importantly* award the scholarships. Create a friendly atmosphere with everyone you contact. You never know who they know or what they know. Never burn your bridges with your peers or adults. The individual you treat badly may be the son or daughter of the person giving out seventy five hundred dollars.

The third venue, and in my personal case, one of the most helpful: books. You need to access as many scholarship, college entry, and college help books that you can find. You do not necessarily need to go buy all of these books because most of them can be checked out from the library. Get all the important details from these books, and TAKE THE TIME to go through them. Focus mainly on scholarship books; this needs to be done in your junior year. You want to create a foundation for yourself so when it comes time for your senior year, you will know exactly how to get the applications, the probable deadlines, and how much each scholarship is offering. Basically, at the beginning of your senior year, all you should have to do is fill out the scholarship, write the essay, and mail in your letters of recommendation.

I always recommend *The Scholarship Book*. This is a very thick book, I would guess about three to five hundred pages full of scholarships. The entire book is filled with nothing but scholarships. I am sure that there are many other books that are just like this one. Do not let this be your beginning and ending source for scholarships, because it is just a foundation. You want to create a vast foundation with numerous books in your collection.

C=COLLECT/CONTACT

When searching for scholarships, you are going to come across a lot of information. You will definitely not be able to remember all of this stuff, so you need to keep physical mementos of what you come across.

When you are looking through a book and you think--you don't even have to be one hundred percent positive that it will help you--but if you even think that the information you see will help you, go straight to the photocopier and copy that page. DO NOT wait until you finish going through the book, because by the time you are done, you will have come across so many different pages with so many different items, that you will forget where half of the stuff is. That could lead you into losing out on some money you could have received. Make a copy of as many pages as you see fit. Keep a journal, just in case you see one sentence on a page and you don't think you will be able to find it later when you look at the copy. In the journal, write down all the important ideas, programs, or Web sites that you think will help in your journey.

When you get on the Web and you find a site that you think may help, print out the page. It is better to print it out and save it for later, because if it has a long Web address and you don't type it exactly to the period, you might not be able to get back to where you were. But when you make a copy of the page, the full Web site will be on the piece of paper and you can easily pull it out and go back.

When talking to people about scholarships, always keep your journal or notebook handy, because they will have some vital information that you will need when you are filling out applications and trying to get recommendations, or just about new places to search for scholarships. It is always helpful for you to have it, because it shows that you have a zeal for your research, and they can truly believe that you are indeed serious about trying to get information. They will value the time spent talking to you more, knowing that you are taking not only mental notes, but also notes on paper about what they are saying. Make sure that you write down, make copies, or print out all the information that you receive. It may be a thousand-dollar scholarship that you forgot because you found a ten thousand-dollar scholarship. It is true that ten thousand dollars is more than one, but when you are dealing with scholarships and getting money, you want to get as much, fill out as much, and receive as much as you can.

H=HELP

Of all the phrases, words of wisdom, and ideas that I have learned, one of the most beneficial is, "The best way to learn something is by teaching it to someone else." When I first heard this saying, I thought to myself, *how can you learn something if you are teaching it to someone else? Don't you have to know it very well already to teach it?* Well this is true in some aspects, but you also have to read between the lines. Basically the saying means that when you are trying to explain something to someone, more ideas about the subject arise in your head, more definition to your subject is identified, and possible venues of solving the problem or completing the search will also be brought up from questions that your "student" asks you. As far as scholarships are concerned, it is true. The more you try to help your friends find scholarships, the better you will become at it. I will explain this further.

Say, for instance, your friend asks you to help them in the search for scholarships, and you know of one book. So you agree to help them and tell them about this book that you know about, and you two decide to go to the library or counseling center (wherever the book is). While searching through the book, you notice that there is a Web site, one you didn't see before when you were searching for your own scholarships. You will start to think, "Wow, another opportunity to find scholarships was right here all the time and I didn't even see it." You go on the 'Net and search for this Web site with your friend, and you find more Web sites that you hadn't seen before. You start coming in contact with all kinds of new information that will help you even more than before. Now, you have gone to the next level. Helping and teaching is learning.

Sometimes it is good to just help someone in need. The saying, "treat a person like you want to be treated," that is so many times abused and misused, is so true. If you knew someone with some information about a scholarship, or anything that you were interested in for that matter, you would want that person to share that information with you. So now it is your turn; be a Good Samaritan, give back to your community with your new words of wisdom and explanation of how to get money for school.

O=ORGANIZE

This section speaks for itself. There is no fine work that is done without fine organization. When you do all of your searching, collect all your information, and help all your friends, you need to organize everything that you receive.

Make a file of all the different scholarship applications that you find. Put them in some kind of order. You can order them by alphabetical order, amount of award, or type of scholarship. You will encounter all kinds of things, so whatever you feel is the best way that you can separate these files and be able to find them in an organized fashion is perfect.

Along with scholarship applications, you will also have letters of recommendation that you need to maintain. Always get a copy of each letter of recommendation that you receive without the signature. This way you can keep all those letters on file and use them again if another scholarship arises. When this does happen, make a copy of the unsigned letter and ask the person to sign the new one. Never have them sign the original, because you always want to have an unsigned copy on file. If the original letter of recommendation is more than four weeks old, scan the original, save the file to a disk, and take it to them so this way they can just change the date and it will save them time. This is pure courtesy, so that they do not have to go through and type a whole new letter of recommendation. Now if you do this and they tell you that they would rather write a new letter than just changing the date, that is fine, but you need to let them make that decision.

Essays are also important documents to keep strictly organized. It is a lot easier to keep your essays organized, because all you have to do is save them on disk. Make sure that they have distinct titles and make sure that you keep that disk. Try to put all of your essays on one disk, because when you start having seven and eight different disks with different information on them, it will be hard to keep up with which files are on which disk. Once you put them on one disk, make one copy of the disk and put it in a safe place, just in case you lose the original. The reason it is so important that you keep up with your disk is because you may be able to use an essay you have already written for another scholarship. This will save you a lot of time, especially if you get into the realm of applying for 20 to 30 scholarships.

For all your information - essays, letters of recommendation, scholarship applications, everything

-once each scholarship package is finally finished, make a copy of your packet. There is nothing worse than filling out all that information and then getting a call about a month later and the person on the other line says, "Hi, I'm calling from the scholarship review board. We got your application, but you forgot to send some paperwork. Before we can review you for the scholarship, we are going to need you to send..." If you hadn't made a copy of your packet, all of your hard work has basically just gone to waste and you are going to have to say, "Can you please send me another application?" By the time you finally get it, they will have already chosen their scholarship recipients. Please don't let this happen to you. If you make a copy of your packet and you get that worrisome phone call--and it can happen, it actually happened to me this summer--but if you receive that call and you have your packet, you can do like I did and reply, "I am sure that I sent everything in, but that is OK, I have a copy of it right here. I can either fax it to you so you will receive it in a few minutes or I can mail it, which would take a few days."

Having that type of organization says something about your personality. It says that you are a proactive troubleshooter and you are prepared for the worst possible occurrences. Organize yourself; this will save you days and days and hours and hours of heartache, headache and stress. If you need to go out and buy an organizer, get a paper organizer, not one of the digital ones to keep phone numbers. You don't even have to buy one of the expensive Franklin's or even Dayminder's, just find something that has months, dates, and a place for you to take notes. This way you can put all the deadlines on it so you can easily remember and plan ahead. You won't have to worry about rushing, because you have created yourself a path to achieve.

L=LEAD

You are a leader. Do not let anyone tell you otherwise. You are a leader, you can accomplish goals, and you can make things happen. Do not wait for someone else to start looking for scholarships before you decide to get on the ball. Do not wait for your parents or counselors to say, "You know, I think it's time that we begin looking for some scholarships for you." It is not their duty or their place to do that. You are the individual planning to go to college. You are the student who does not want to pay for your education. You want to be able to say that you got some money back because you had an ample amount of scholarships. It is all about you. Start your search as soon as possible. It is never too early and it is never too late. When I say never, I mean never. You can begin searching in middle school, or you can begin searching if you are planning to go to college and it has been ten years since you were last in school. There is no time limit on this issue, and don't let anyone tell you that there is. I want you to utilize those leadership skills that you have deep within you. I want other students to look at you and say, "Wow, you are dedicated to making sure you go to school for free, maybe I should do that."

As I have previously stated, when they come up to you and ask how you are doing all of this, I want you to help them. You will be surprised by how many people become interested in you because they can see your zeal for excellence. You may find yourself giving counselors advice on how to advise other students about scholarships. Don't let anything stop you from your goal, and do not, under any circumstances forget what your goal is: **Go to school without having to pay a penny out of your pocket**. Keep that in mind the whole time that you are searching. Let that be your motivation and driving force to that freedom of bills that you will acquire upon entering that college or university. Leaders are rewarded for their skills.

A=ACTIVATE

You have to activate yourself to take on what comes to you. When you first look at the scholarship applications, the first thought that will come to your mind is how big the application packet is. Some of them will be one page and that's it. But some of them will be eight to ten pages. Don't let this discourage you in any form or fashion. Stride through these applications, but take slow strides. You want to make sure that you fill out each section to the best of your ability and with the most recent information about yourself that you can include. In the section, "awards, honors, etc." list all activities where you have been honored. It doesn't matter if it is the honor roll, your church, your team, or your teacher that honored you. Include all of that, even though you may think that it wasn't a big deal and that the particular ceremony or function wasn't important enough for you to include in your application. It is, use it. You must use all that you have in your past to help boost your future.

Spend time thinking about your essay before you write it. I can't stress this enough. Your essay is the place where the scholarship review board meets the real you. Most essays will ask you questions like "What career do you want and why?", "What are your long-term and short-term goals and why?", "What are you going to major in and why?". They are usually very general questions about your plans for the future, and they want to see how deeply you can back it up. Basically they are trying to see how badly you want to achieve your specific goals, how much you have researched your plans, and how well you have planned out your future. They want to choose the person they believe will be the best benefactor of their scholarship. In other words, they want to support an individual they believe will succeed. That individual is you!

Once you activate, your words will flow smoothly, your essays will be forthright, and your plans for your future will be right. Activate yourself; take yourself to the next level of thinking. Go to the place where it doesn't matter how long it takes you to finally finish that application; where you don't mind asking your teachers, principals, and even past or present employers to write that letter of recommendation. Become activated so that you have more than enough motivation to spend hours seeking, collecting, helping, organizing, and leading. Do this and you will get...

R=RESULTS

Once you have searched, collected, helped, organized, led, and activated, you will get results. Scholarships will come banging down your door because you spent time to actually go out and get what you wanted. You stayed dedicated and worked hard during those meticulous hours of searching. You stayed steady on your goal and stayed focused on completing what you were searching for, and you have gained a college education at no financial debt to you or your family. How does it feel to finally be walking on the college campus? Feel the breeze? Inhale…exhale. Smell that fresh air. When the twentieth class day, or whatever deadline your university chooses comes, and other students are scurrying around campus trying to figure out how they are going to pay for this semester. You can relax. Your college is paid for. Enjoy earning your degree financially free.

About the Author

Charles J. Phillips is originally from Lansing, Michigan. He graduated from Prairie View A&M University with a Bachelor's of Science degree in Chemical Engineering, and is currently an Engineer for E.I. du Pont de Nemours & Co. Inc in Parkersburg, West Virginia. Motivated by the fact his parents did not have the money to pay for his college; Charles spent a tremendous amount of his sophomore through senior years of high school preparing for a free education. He not only earned enough scholarships to pay for all four years of college, he actually earned more than required and had extra spending money.

Printed in the United States
47532LVS00001B/219